EBURY PRESS
THE MANIFESTATION BLUEPRINT

Him-eesh Madaan is one of India's leading mindset coaches and content creators, on a mission to help people reprogramme their thinking and design a life they truly deserve.

From selling one-rupee jaljeera on the streets to inspiring millions globally, his journey is a testament to what happens when belief meets action. Over the past twelve-plus years, he has impacted more than 10 million lives through his content, coaching and live sessions, building a loyal community of 11 million+ followers across platforms and 1 billion+ views.

As the host of the Him-eesh Madaan Podcast, he has had insightful conversations with leading entrepreneurs and changemakers, such as Ritesh Agarwal (OYO), Aman Gupta (boAt), Ghazal Alagh (Mamaearth), Anupam Mittal (People Group), Dr Arokiaswamy Velumani (Thyrocare), Aakash Anand (Bella Vita Organic), Padma Shri Awardee Chef Sanjeev Kapoor, Gurudev Sri Sri Ravi Shankar, HG Amogh Lila Prabhu, Swami Mukundananda and many more.

Through these interactions, Him-eesh discovered one common thread among all: the power of a resilient and growth-oriented mindset that turns ordinary beginnings into extraordinary success.

Recipient of the Nelson Mandela Nobel Peace Award (2021) and an honorary doctorate, Him-eesh has also worked with leading organizations, such as Paytm, Sony, SBI, Hero and IITs, and has been featured on CNBC, CNN, *Economic Times*, *Dainik Bhaskar* and *Jagran*.

In *The Manifestation Blueprint*, he combines science, psychology and personal experience to reveal the scientific secrets to manifesting success, showing readers how to rewire their inner world to transform their outer reality.

THE MANIFESTATION
BLUEPRINT

Turn Your Thoughts into Reality

HIM-EESH MADAAN

EBURY
PRESS

An imprint of Penguin Random House

EBURY PRESS

Ebury Press is an imprint of the Penguin Random House group of companies whose addresses can be found at global.penguinrandomhouse.com

Published by Penguin Random House India Pvt. Ltd
4th Floor, Capital Tower 1, MG Road,
Gurugram 122 002, Haryana, India

First published in Ebury Press by Penguin Random House India 2025

Copyright © Him-eesh Madaan 2025

All rights reserved

10 9 8 7 6 5 4 3 2 1

The views and opinions expressed in this book are the author's own and the facts are as reported by him which have been verified to the extent possible, and the publishers are not in any way liable for the same.

Please note that no part of this book may be used or reproduced in any manner for the purpose of training artificial intelligence technologies or systems.

ISBN 9780143466246

Typeset in Bembo Std by MAP Systems, Bengaluru, India
Printed at Thomson Press India Ltd, New Delhi

This book is sold subject to the condition that it shall not, by way of trade or otherwise, be lent, resold, hired out or otherwise circulated without the publisher's prior consent in any form of binding or cover other than that in which it is published and without a similar condition including this condition being imposed on the subsequent purchaser.

www.penguin.co.in

Contents

Introduction: I Photoshopped My Life   vii

1. The Invisible Forces   1
2. Four Myths of Happiness   15
3. Your Mindset Drives You   33
4. Seven Fundamentals of Growth Mindset   49
5. From Confusion to Clarity   83
6. The Engine Behind Your Goals   105
7. Manifestation Decoded   123
8. The Magic of Momentum   147
9. Daily Mastery: 21 Days   159

Introduction

I Photoshopped My Life

On 25 December 2018, I was reflecting on the previous year. I had been working hard for the last few years but had not been able to create much financial progress in my life. During this introspection, I unearthed some magical elements that had influenced my life positively but had remained under-utilized. Now, as the new year approached, I started writing down all my aspirations with renewed hope and determination. They weren't just 'New Year's Goals'—I named them my 'New Life Goals'!

As 1 January 2019 dawned, I made a WhatsApp group with myself. I downloaded a few images from the Internet and even edited some of them to suit my purpose. **These were the images of objects and places that seemed out of my reach at that time, but I dared to make them my goals.**

This part of my life is personal and could lead to judgment, but in this book, I want to be 100 per cent transparent with you as I believe that my journey, filled with a touch of madness and a step-by-step approach, can inspire and help you lead the life you desire.

One of my aspirations was to buy two Apple watches—one for me, one for my wife—and a MacBook for my work. So, I downloaded an image of a couple wearing Apple watches and sent it to my WhatsApp group along with the photo of a MacBook.

Another dream involved owning a Mercedes—not for external validation, but for deeply personal reasons related to a childhood experience. So, I even photoshopped a picture of a Mercedes car alongside us.

I also envisioned the type of house where my family would live and found an image on the Internet that matched my vision. Anyone can call this act as 'foolish'. It won't be wrong in saying, 'If you don't have money to buy an Apple watch, you don't dream to own a luxury car or a house.'

And yes, as a coach and trainer, I aspired to deliver TED talks too.

My childhood was marked by financial hardships, and I never believed I'd have the opportunity to travel outside of India. However, my wife, Gunjan, came from a family that travelled to some parts of the country annually. I photoshopped an image to place me and my wife in front of Sydney's Opera House.

As I was never able to go to college because of financial constraints, my wife and I wanted to contribute to the education of others. Hence, we resolved to fund the education of at least 100 students. My other goals included freedom to work from anywhere, a nice office for my team, a fit body, and many more.

Now, let me share the results.

I was able to achieve 100 per cent of my goals using the fundamentals I am going to discuss in this book.

Even the goals which were 100x of my financial worth, even the goals which sounded impossible to many—I was able to achieve them all.

2019: We got Apple watches and my MacBook.

2020: We moved to a nice office.

2021: We moved to a beautiful house and bought a Mercedes.

2022: I delivered my first TED talk and worked from Goa for a fortnight.

2023: We funded the education of 100 students, took a 'one-way' flight to Australia, visited the Oprah House, clicked the **exact** same picture as I had photoshopped and worked from Australia for a month. In 2024, we worked from the US for a month, and then in 2025, visited four new countries.

How Did This Happen?

When I was twelve, my family lost everything. We were deep in debt, and for the next eight to nine years, life was nothing short of a storm. It was during this time that I learned some of the greatest lessons about attitude and mindset—how to smile through setbacks, how to stay hopeful when everything falls apart and how to rebuild piece by piece. Because of financial constraints, I couldn't attend college and started working right after school at seventeen. Years later, when we were able to rebuild everything, I realized that every breakthrough—every change—began in the mind. That realization became my mission. I decided to quit my aviation career and chose to become a life coach so I could help others realize their potential, find happiness and experience the transformation.

Being in this field gave me the privilege of closely studying the lives of numerous successful people, working with CEOs, training major corporations and impacting thousands of individuals. Through these experiences, I discovered what truly works—and what doesn't.

By 2019, I had already achieved some milestones, but I wanted to test the power of manifestation for myself. So, I decided to set goals that were bigger, bolder and beyond logic—goals that would challenge me, bring out my best and add new dimensions to my life. (I'll share more about this journey in the chapters ahead.)

Why Did I Write This Book?

After working diligently to create value in people's lives through workshops and videos, I still felt there could be more.

There has to be a more comprehensive solution that is handy and accessible

Hence, the book that is in your hands—to help you live your life to the fullest.

Don't mistake this book as just the tale of my personal success; it's a road map for you to follow. It can prove to be a game changer for you.

This book isn't going to give you any fancy theories or impossible-to-follow advice. It's like having a real friend next to you, one who gets the struggles and the dreams just like you have. Each page is filled with practical steps, simple actions and relatable stories that can turn your dreams into realities.

Why Should You Read This Book?

You might be wondering this right now. Here's the answer—every single chapter is designed with YOU in mind. This book is going to help you get clarity about your goals, teach you simple but powerful tricks to improve yourself and give you ideas to tackle the same problems, but with a fresh perspective. It will feel like having a chat with a mentor who truly understands you. I can say that because I have been through the same life myself and I have been able to break through.

Whether you're striving for professional success, personal growth or simply a happier life, this book will guide you on your journey through the fundamental principles outlined here.

Once you start studying yourself—understanding your thoughts and patterns—you will find that *it is the difference that will create a difference in your life*. From there, you will start getting clarity and then, creating a guide, a blueprint for your own life.

My goal is that when you finish this book, you don't just walk away with clarity or confidence—you walk away transformed, with a new mindset, a new energy and a new way of looking at yourself and your future.

Always remember why you decided to read this book. That is your first step to a successful life. Keep that intention close to your heart and it will propel you forward by giving you a purpose and the required motivation.

Ready to make a change?

Let's dive in to take this journey to the best version of yourself. Happy learning!

Chapter 1

The Invisible Forces

Imagine spending all your life learning from your surroundings—your family, schools, colleges and various institutions—but you are never taught about mindset or the power of the mind. It's like operating a complex machine without any training. As a result, we face issues like communicating feelings, frustration, anger, depression, procrastination and even laziness.

Think about it. Every new employee gets thorough training before operating a machine to ensure maximum efficiency. But the irony is that *we navigate life without any training for our mind, a machine far more complex than any man-made device.*

We think constantly—from the moment we wake up till we fall asleep, and even in our dreams. Every emotion we feel, every decision we make, every success or setback we experience is born from a single source—our thoughts. Yet, how often do we pause to understand *how* we think?

We upgrade our phones, cars and skills, but rarely upgrade the one system that drives it all—the mind.

We spend a lifetime using this machine, but never truly learn to operate it.

I once heard a beautiful analogy:

When force is applied to an egg from the outside, a life ends. But when the same egg experiences force, pressure and energy from within, a life is created. The egg remains unchanged, yet the **source** *of the force makes all the difference.*

Humans work in the same way.

The first element in the process of changing your life story is understanding the forces that shape our actions, decisions, and ultimately, our destiny. Everything we achieve, every breakthrough we experience, begins in the mind before it manifests in reality.

Take a moment to think: What's the most essential element for survival? Oxygen. We can't see it, yet every breath depends on it.

Have you ever noticed that the most important things in life are often invisible?

The same goes for emotions and energy. They shape our lives in profound ways, though they remain unseen.

The same goes for electricity—you can't touch it or see it moving, but it powers everything around you. And think about Wi-Fi signals. You can't see them, yet they connect you instantly to the world.

Love is another example. You can feel it, express it and experience its power, but you can't physically see it.

Now, consider a giant tree. You admire its tall branches reaching for the sky, the rustle of its leaves, the fruits it bears and the cool shade it offers on a hot day. But pause for a moment and ask yourself—what truly sustains this tree? What makes it strong enough to stand through storms, heat and seasons of change?

It's the roots, hidden deep underground. You never see them, yet they hold the entire tree together. They draw nourishment, give stability and keep it alive. The stronger the roots, the stronger the tree.

The same is true for us. Our **inner world**—our beliefs, thoughts, mindset, emotions and attitude—is our root. And our **outer world**—our relationships, confidence, wealth, peace and personality—is the fruit.

Whatever we experience on the outside—success or struggle, happiness or stress, courage or fear—is simply a reflection of what lies beneath. If your roots are weak, the fruit will eventually wither. But when you nourish your inner world, your outer world flourishes effortlessly.

Yet most people do the opposite. They keep polishing the fruit while ignoring the roots. They switch jobs, change partners, try new habits or wardrobes—constantly looking for external fixes, while the real solution lies within.

Your confidence, your peace of mind, your financial stability, your resilience—all these are branches growing from the same root: your mindset. When you strengthen your roots, everything else begins to bloom.

Across cultures and scriptures, the wisdom of the 'roots and fruits' runs deep. The Upanishads and the Bhagavad Gita speak of the **Ashvattha Tree**. It reminds us that the unseen roots (our inner world) sustain the visible branches (our outer life). Similarly, the Bible teaches, *'A tree is known by its fruit'*—emphasizing that our inner faith and values determine the quality of our actions and outcomes.

Whether through ancient vedic philosophy or biblical wisdom, the message remains timeless: **when you nurture your roots, your fruits naturally flourish.** Simple, yet life-changing.

So, make it your mission to nourish your inner world—your thoughts, your beliefs your emotions—and watch how the outer world begins to mirror that growth.

Why Beliefs Matter?

Try answering these questions:

- How do you feel most of the time—good or unsettled?
- How easily do you bounce back when things go wrong?
- Do you believe you have untapped potential within you?
- How often do you think with clarity and how often does it turn into overthinking?
- Do your daily choices come from confidence or from the need for approval?
- If no one were watching, would you still chase the same goals?

Now that you have thought of the answers to each question, let me tell you this.

Since childhood, there are a few beliefs that we all are given, then there are other beliefs that we create from our environment and observations. There are hundreds of reasons why each one of these beliefs are created.

After years of observing people around me and asking countless questions during training sessions, I finally understood how my personality took shape and how I became the person I am today. With this realization came the power to make intentional changes.

For example, I noticed patterns in my family. My grandmother is an overthinker, my aunt often struggles with anxiety, and my father has battled it for years. I was determined to break free from this cycle. At the same time, I also recognized the **positive traits** I had inherited.

Confidence runs strong in my family, and I made sure to hold on to that strength.

Our beliefs are shaped by the environment we grow up in. From childhood, we unconsciously absorb the thoughts, habits and emotions of those around us. The way our parents react to challenges, the fears they hold, the values they cherish—all of these become ingrained in us before we even realize it.

We pick up ideas about success, failure, love and self-worth from our family, teachers and society. If we are raised in an environment that fosters confidence and resilience, we naturally develop a strong mindset. On the other hand, if we grow up in a space filled with doubt, anxiety or limitations, these patterns often shape our subconscious beliefs, influencing how we approach life.

However, our beliefs are not set in stone. We have the power to reshape them. Unless we actively seek new experiences, engage with learned individuals, read thought-provoking books and challenge our thought patterns, our beliefs remain confined to what we have always known. Growth happens when we step beyond the familiar, question old assumptions and consciously choose what to believe.

Understanding this is going to be the first step towards transforming your mindset and creating a life you truly desire. The moment you realize that you can rewrite your own narrative, you begin to break free from inherited limitations and step into a world of new possibilities. To understand this deeply, let's look at two powerful examples: money and public speaking

The Money Belief

Money is often seen as the root of bad behaviour, negative attitudes and many problems in life. When someone struggles financially, they may pass down negative views about money to their children, rather than teaching how money, when used wisely, can bring growth and comfort.

Let me give you an example to make this clearer.

When we moved to our current neighbourhood, we already had certain **assumptions** about the people living there. Seeing expensive cars parked outside their homes, we believed they would be cold-hearted and arrogant simply because they were wealthy. But as we got to know them, we realized how warm, kind and genuine they were, just like anyone else. Our belief about rich people was completely shaken.

This experience showed us how **powerful and deeply ingrained** beliefs can be. Imagine a child growing up with the idea that having more money than you need is bad. Over time, this belief can unconsciously shape their decisions, making them feel guilty about financial success, hesitant to charge their worth or even afraid to pursue ambitious goals. Without realizing it, they may limit their potential simply because of a belief they never questioned.

Now think about another child who grows up in a home where money is always a source of tension—parents arguing about expenses, relatives fighting over inheritance or constant talk about how 'money ruins relationships'.

Even without anyone saying it directly, the child starts linking *money* with *stress*. As they grow older, every time they think about earning more, investing or managing finances, that old emotion resurfaces. Their body tenses, their mind hesitates—not because they lack capability, but because somewhere deep inside, money feels unsafe.

On the other hand, a child raised in an environment where wealth is seen as a reward for effort and creativity develops a very different emotional blueprint. For them, money represents freedom, growth and possibility. They enjoy talking about it, earning it and multiplying it because to them, money feels natural.

This is why challenging and reshaping our beliefs is essential. The mind holds onto ideas as truths until we put them to the test. Only when we consciously examine them can we break free from the limitations they create.

Public Speaking

Another common example is the fear of public speaking. Think back to a time in school when a student stood up to answer a question. The teacher cross-questioned them and the class erupted in laughter. That student might not remember the courage it took to speak up, but in that moment, a silent decision was made—never to stand up and risk being ridiculed. That's how stage fear can begin.

Now, take a step back and reflect.

Do you remember other people's mistakes on stage? Probably not. And just like that, most people don't remember yours either.

It's not the audience that holds us back—it's the belief we created about ourselves. The fear of public speaking isn't about the stage or the people watching; it's about the story we've told ourselves about what will happen if we speak up.

Here's the truth: we can rewrite our story.

Confidence isn't the absence of fear. It's the decision to not let fear control us. When we challenge our limiting beliefs, we realize that the only thing standing in our way is the belief that I can't. And the moment we decide otherwise, everything changes.

Whatever we are today is a result of the belief system we developed over time—through our parents, friends, surroundings and environment. We observed, learned and formed empowering or limiting beliefs.

In this chapter, we explored *how* beliefs are formed. In the chapters ahead, we'll uncover *what* they do—especially one belief that almost everyone misunderstands: the belief about **happiness**. Because the biggest transformation in life doesn't happen when you change *what* you do . . . it happens when you understand *why* you do it.

In the next chapter, using the **5 Whys**, we'll dig deeper—layer by layer—until we reach that one root belief that silently drives your choices, emotions and destiny. And when we reach Chapter 7, we'll go even deeper—learning how to identify, reprogram and replace limiting beliefs with ones that make you unstoppable.

Your roots are already at work—shaping your thoughts, your actions, your future. The only question is: are they helping you grow . . . or keeping you from becoming the tree you were meant to be?

Conclusion

This chapter has shown us that belief isn't just a concept; it's the engine that drives our life's journey. It is like the secret ingredient in a recipe, the magic that turns an ordinary dish into an extraordinary feast. It's not just about hoping for the best—it's about knowing, deep down, that you have the power to shape your reality, just like the force applied on an 'egg'. When the force comes from within, it can create miracles.

Beliefs are the unseen but crucial roots that sustain us. We often try to fix our external world without realizing that the real change happens within.

If you want to see different fruits, you need to nourish the roots. Confidence, happiness and success—they all stem from a strong inner belief system.

Chapter 2

Four Myths of Happiness

The 5 Whys Method

One of the most effective ways to uncover the true cause of a problem is the **5 Whys Method**. Let's understand this method with a fascinating real-life example.

The caretakers of the Washington Monument were concerned about the high maintenance costs incurred to keep it clean. Instead of making assumptions, they conducted a detailed analysis by digging into the problem. They did it by repeatedly asking *why* until they reached the **root cause**. Here's how their inquiry unfolded:

1. **Why does cleaning the monument cost so much?**
   Because pigeons frequently sit on it, making it dirty.
2. **Why do pigeons sit on the monument?**
   Because they come to eat the spiders living there.
3. **Why are there so many spiders?**
   Because they are drawn to the mosquitoes swarming around the monument.

4. **Why does the monument attract mosquitoes?**
   Because the lights, which are switched on *before* sunset, attract them.
5. **Why aren't the lights switched on *at* sunset instead?**
   That hadn't been considered before.

With this simple yet powerful questioning approach, they discovered that the timing of the monument's lights was the root cause of the problem.

The solution: Delaying the lights until after sunset significantly reduced the mosquito population, which in turn, lowered the presence of spiders and pigeons. Ultimately, this resulted in cutting down the high cleaning costs.

Applying the 5 Whys to Your Life

The goal of the 5 Whys isn't to stop at surface-level answers but to keep questioning until you reach the real cause of any issue. Whether it's a personal challenge, a career roadblock or an emotional setback, asking *why* repeatedly helps you dig deeper and find the true reason behind your struggles.

Remember, it's not about asking *exactly* five questions—you may find the root cause sooner or need to ask a few more.

The key is to keep going until you uncover the answer that truly drives change.

The 'Why' Behind Everything in Life

Understanding the root of our desires and actions can be eye-opening. Have you ever paused to think about why you do the things you do? Why do you pursue certain goals? Often, at the core, it's about seeking happiness. We might associate happiness with specific achievements or possessions, believing that attaining them will bring us joy. But does it really?

Let's understand this better.

Imagine your ambition is to buy a new house. Now, let's use the '5 Whys' method to explore this further:

1. **Why do I want to buy a new house?**
   Because I wish to live in a bigger and better place.
2. **Why do I wish to live in a bigger and better place?**
   Because I think it will give me a better lifestyle.
3. **Why do I want a better lifestyle?**
   Because a better lifestyle will give me validation and positive emotions.
4. **Why do I associate a new house with validation and positive emotions?**
   Because it signifies achievement and success.

5. **Why do I seek achievement and success?**
   Because ultimately, I believe it will make me happy.

This exercise demonstrates that at the root of every desire is the pursuit of happiness. This simple desire, when unravelled, reveals the fundamental truth about human motivation—we do everything in the pursuit of happiness

Even acts that seem selfless are motivated by the satisfaction we derive from helping others.

Consider this:
- You donate money to help children get an education. Why? Because seeing them succeed makes you happy.
- You aspire to get married. Why? Because you believe having a partner will bring you happiness.

Myth #1: The Mirage of Money

Have you ever noticed how young professionals spend their first salaries? They rush to buy expensive phones, watches and other luxuries, believing that these purchases will bring them happiness and fulfilment. But how long does that happiness really last?

Let's take the story of a couple who fought constantly. They were convinced that the root of their unhappiness was their small, rented home. They believed that once they bought their own dream house, all problems would vanish. When they finally got the keys, the joy was immense. The first few days were full of laughter, celebrations and peace. But soon, arguments crept back—this time within the walls of the very home they thought would bring permanent happiness.

The house had provided temporary excitement, not permanent solution to happiness. Associating happiness with a car, phone, house or other such material goals will keep you waiting to be happy forever. What it provides is momentary excitement, not lasting happiness. As soon as you accomplish one goal, you'll be searching for a new one to regain that feeling.

The Truth About Money and Happiness

Let's be clear: **money is important.**

I value comfort, and I work tirelessly to provide a good life for myself and those around me. I do not undermine the significance of financial security because I know how it feels to struggle for essentials—medical expenses, college fees or even pocket money for the canteen. I know it because I have lived it all during my childhood.

Money is not an evil. It's a necessity. But the key is understanding why you desire money, possessions or luxuries.

If you peel the layers of this desire using the 5 Whys, they all lead to one word—*happiness*. Why you want that car, why you want that watch, why you want financial success. Once you find the answer to your why, you will see that it will always lead you to one ultimate goal: happiness.

Now, people often say: 'What is the need to build wealth, as many wealthy people decide to quit worldly pleasures after becoming millionaires or billionaires?' But that is not true. Not every billionaire or a wealthy person quits. There are people who happily become wealthy. They find joy in small achievements, with their families, and with every step of growth in their lives.

So, rather than chasing objects, chase the feeling behind them. Because happiness is not something you buy; it's something you cultivate.

Myth #2: The Accomplishment Trap

From a young age, we are victims of a scam due to which society conditions us to delay happiness. Think of it. There's always a condition to be fulfilled to become happy.

- 'Achieve success in your tenth exam, and the pleasures of life will follow.'
- 'Excel in your twelfth exam first, and then the joys of life will embrace you.'
- 'Get into a good college, then you'll be happy.'
- 'Secure a good job, and life will be fulfilling.'
- 'Get married, and happiness will follow.'

This pattern continues with every milestone you achieve, pushing the promise of happiness further and further into a future that seemingly never arrives. Each step is portrayed as the key to happiness, yet once achieved, it often leads to the next goalpost, preventing us from truly enjoying the present.

Why do we chase accomplishments? For recognition.

Why recognition? For self-worth.

Why self-worth? Because we think *then* we'll be happy.

It's about appreciating the present moment and finding joy in the here and now, not in future achievements or possessions.

I'm not suggesting you abandon your goals or desires. Accomplishments have their place and can enhance our lives. However, it's important to recognize that happiness is a state of being, not a destination.

Think about it. Challenge your beliefs. Open your mind to the possibility that happiness can be found in everyday moments, independent of accomplishments or assets.

Happiness Is Now

You might find it confusing in the beginning. You might think that I am asking you to not associate your happiness with accomplishments while I myself earn well, and I spend well too. Just a few days ago, I celebrated my accomplishment and thanked my audience for 8 million subscribers on YouTube.

There is an important point worth mentioning here.

If you keep on waiting for accomplishments to feel happy, you are missing the joy of living your life. You can't be limitless like this.

You will always have limits to happiness, to growth. What I feel and try to live every day is what I want you to do too. Remind yourself each day to enjoy the journey.

How? Let me explain.

Your goal is to reach Manali from say, Delhi, covering a distance of 575.8 kms by road. As it generally happens, you set the destination on Google Maps. You will notice a lot of places along the path indicated on the map, the milestones that will come along the way.

But if you believe happiness lies *only* in reaching Manali, you'll miss the magic that unfolds along the way. Imagine starting your drive in the soft morning light, the city slowly fading behind you. As the road opens up, you stop at a famous dhaba near Murthal for parathas and chai. A few hours later, the air turns cooler, the scenery shifts and you roll down your windows to let the mountain breeze in. You take a quick break by the Beas river, dip your feet in the cold water, order a bowl of steaming Maggi and watch the sunlight dance on the waves. The playlist hits your favourite track, laughter fills the car and every turn brings a new view—a waterfall here, a pine forest there, maybe even a rainbow after light rain.

That's the beauty of the journey. If you keep your eyes only on the destination, you miss the dhabas, the laughter, the music, the smell of rain and the countless small moments that make the trip unforgettable.

This is why enjoying the journey is just as important as reaching the destination.

Your life is also similar. Every small occurrence or incident can be a joyful experience in itself. Enjoy all of it to take the full measure of life and attain happiness.

Aimlessly working doesn't help you achieve that.

We are Human Beings, Not Human Doings! If you keep on doing without feeling, it's not worth it.

Now take a moment to analyse. Think along the following lines:

- How many times did you deprive yourself a chance to be happy because of this relation you have created in your mind?
- How many times did you delay it and did not enjoy the journey because you were busy getting worried about your end goal?

Myth #3: The Approval Illusion

I remember one of my one-to-one coaching clients, a bright young man who came to me appearing calm and successful. On paper, everything about him looked perfect—he had a stable corporate job, a decent salary and his parents were proud of him. Yet as we began our conversations, I sensed a strange emptiness in his words.

So, I asked him to walk me through his journey. That's when the real story unfolded. He told me he had always dreamt of starting his own business. He had ideas he couldn't stop thinking about—scribbled plans hidden away in notebooks, sketches of logos, late-night market research he never showed anyone. But when the time came to choose his path, his parents were worried about the risks. They wanted him to have a secure career, something they could proudly talk about with relatives.

And so, to keep them happy, he took the corporate job. Every achievement at work brought him praise from his family but not joy. He smiled on the outside while quietly mourning the dreams he had buried inside. The weight of their happiness sat on his shoulders like an invisible load. He wasn't failing in life, but he was failing himself.

That's when we realized something crucial: he wasn't unhappy because of the job itself—he was unhappy because he was **living for others' happiness, not his own.**

He might look happy to everyone, but in most of such cases, emotions are being suppressed inside. There is a negative energy built-up within. They might think they are happy with the choices they have made, but that is not the truth. Such suppression leads to anger, depression and anxiety. It is like a tiny Band-Aid on a serious wound—the wrong treatment. It's temporary. It can create further damage. Band-Aids are used for small cuts. Wounds need to be properly cured.

Ignoring yourself and thinking about the happiness of others is not going to lead you anywhere. I also agree that it is important to take the feelings of your family into account. But understand one thing—if you are not happy, it is not possible for you to keep your family, or anyone else, happy.

You Can't Give What You Don't Have

If I have no money in my pocket, how can I give even a penny to anyone? If I have a 100-rupee note, I can lend a portion, or all of it. But if I don't have any money of my own, it is impossible for me to give or share my money with anyone.

So, if you are trying to create happiness in your life by making compromises, you can't do it. You have to take care of your happiness so that you 'feel' happy and can spread and share that happiness in the lives of those around you.

I am not saying that you should not spend money on the people you love or share your finances. What I mean is that you can support your family financially and you can spend quality time with them. Nevertheless, sacrificing your happiness is not an option.

In fact, I want you to adopt this attitude: 'I am earning well. I am always there for my family unconditionally—personally and financially. *But my own happiness is important.*'

Happiness should not be dependent on others.

Myth #4: The Scarcity Lie

A lot of people believe that happiness is limited. 'We can't stay happy all the time.' Reflect on your own life. Maybe happiness isn't as restricted as you think.

We've been conditioned from childhood to believe that constant happiness is unattainable.

A father I coached believed that parenting had to involve constant stress, scolding and discipline. 'If I'm always calm, they'll never listen,' he said. He decided to test this belief—he shifted to calm, respectful conversations while still being firm. Within weeks, the tension at home dropped. He realized joy and discipline can co-exist, and that happiness wasn't something to be rationed.

One of my entrepreneur friends believed stress was the price of success. He assumed life had to be a rollercoaster. But when he finally took a two-week break and created structure in his business, he found he could be productive *and* peaceful. It shocked him—happiness didn't have to be rare or occasional. The key point is to challenge the beliefs around happiness you've been taught.

We're often told happiness is limited, and we follow this notion without questioning it. Right from the beginning, we are all conditioned to not be happy all the time. When you were laughing in class, the teacher pointed you out. When a person comes home smiling ear to ear, they are commented upon with suspicion and discomfort. We are so conditioned that we start questioning happiness itself.

My point here is that happiness is not limited—that's just an assumption. I can prove that you can access happiness whenever and wherever you want. Just like our sadness is generated from our thoughts, happiness is also generated from our thoughts.

Try this experiment right now: close your eyes and think of all the beautiful things and events in your life for which you are grateful. Consider the blessings you have—a roof over your head, food on your plate and family who cares for you. Reflect on the moments that made you feel happy, proud and grateful. Do these memories make you feel happy? If yes, then you've accessed happiness by your own choice.

Conclusion

No matter how many goals you make with a negative mind, they can never be achieved. There is a science behind it all. One can't be creative with a negative mindset. You can't have ideas, solve problems, face challenges or be emotionally strong. When you pursue growth and seek comfort in your life, but your mind keeps turning towards negativity, you become sad and depressed easily. You keep postponing your happiness instead of feeling joy in the little things. You break down again and again. That is why, if you are not happy, no goals can be achieved. And even if you manage to achieve them somehow, you can't retain them. But when you are happy, your creativity, imagination, resilience, consistency, problem-solving skills, persistence, commitment, thought process and strength—all keep enhancing.

Keep trying and keep accomplishing your goals, but instead of being happy only after achieving them, be happy throughout that process of achievement.

Don't wait for life's milestones to bring you happiness. Embrace happiness today, in every moment and in every simple joy. Remember, happiness is not about waiting for the storm to pass but about learning to dance in the rain.

So, the next time you find yourself chasing after the next big thing, take a moment to reflect and appreciate what you already have in your possession. True happiness is within your reach, right here, right now.

Chapter 3

Your Mindset Drives You

The Day Everything Changed

6 December 1999.
I still remember that day vividly, as if the air itself had turned heavy.

We were a happy family in Amritsar. My father ran a flourishing business. Life felt secure, full of promise. He believed in doing everything with honesty and integrity, never cutting corners, never bending his ethics. He trusted that goodness always wins in the end.

But that day, everything collapsed.

Competitors who couldn't match his values chose shortcuts. They used political influence, fabricated false cases and unleashed chaos on our lives. Our office was stormed by goons. There were threats, lies and negative news everywhere. The media painted us as villains. Police turned their backs. Overnight, everything we owned—our business, our assets, even our peace—was snatched away.

Worse than losing everything was **not knowing if my parents were even alive.** We had to scatter for safety. I was sent to my maternal grandparents' house. My brother stayed with an aunt. My parents went into hiding.

I remember lying on a small bed in my grandparents' home, hearing them whisper in the next room, their voices trembling:

'What if they can't take it anymore? What if they . . . do something to themselves?'

Every phone ring felt like doom. Every knock on the door made my heart stop.

Then one day, after what felt like forever, I saw my father again. And he was smiling.

No fear on his face. No bitterness in his eyes. Just calm courage. He looked at us and said, **'We will not give up. We will rebuild everything.'** And he meant it.

Rising from Ruins

The next ten years became our battlefield. We started from zero—even below zero, buried under debts and disgrace. We as a family did everything to clear our debts. From selling one-rupee jaljeera on the streets of Amritsar to selling nut milk made by my mother and grandmother, we did whatever it took to survive.

Eventually, a few years down, we moved to Delhi and each of us took up jobs just to keep going. I was not able to go to college, so I took a job at a travel agency for Rs 2500 and then did multiple jobs. Each one of us worked hard and excelled in our respective careers. Slowly, brick by brick, we rebuilt our lives.

But here's what still amazes me: In the same kind of situation, I've heard of people giving up . . . even ending their lives. Yet my father never sank. He never let despair enter his mind. He smiled, he fought and he stayed rooted in his values.

And there was one thing he never stopped doing: **feeding his mind.**

Even in the darkest days, he read books on attitude and personal growth, attended mindset trainings and filled his mind with strength when life gave him none.

The Birth of My Obsession

Watching my family rise from the ashes changed me forever. It made me realize something profound: **Mindset is the real foundation of life.**

You can lose your wealth, your job, or your assets—but if your mindset is strong, you can rebuild it all and even build something greater than before.

That is why, thirteen years ago, I chose to speak about mindset on YouTube when nobody was watching and there was no money in it. Even if only 100 people watched my videos in a whole month, I was happy because I wasn't chasing views. I was chasing *change*.

That is why I left my corporate job, and that is why I am here today. Because I have lived what mindset can do. I have seen it turn rock bottom into a launchpad.

This is my why. This is why I will never stop talking about mindset. Because I know it can save lives. It saved my family.

If I am able to instil the right mindset in you, all the preceding events of your life will have a 'ripple effect'. Look at a successful man's life—not only renowned personalities like Dr A.P.J. Abdul Kalam, Ratan Tata or Dhirubhai Ambani, but even your next-door neighbour, to see how they have constantly evolved and bettered their circumstances. The lady who has been juggling various jobs and is still able to look after her children and family well, the man who has been able to earn better for his family and give good education to his children—they are equally successful as the big names.

If you listen to public sports figures like Mahendra Singh Dhoni, Virat Kohli, Rohit Sharma, Cristiano Ronaldo, etc., they all give the whole credit to mindset only. So, what kind of mindset are we talking about here?

It's Neither Fixed Mindset, Nor Growth Mindset

Whenever I attended any training programme, I always asked this question to my trainers: why does it have to be either fixed or growth, isn't it a journey? This one question changed many trainers' curriculums. People say that you have a fixed mindset or a growth mindset, a negative mindset or a positive mindset. But I say no to this. I believe it is a journey.

You might trouble yourself thinking you have a fixed mindset or a growth mindset, but you can have a different mindset depending on your circumstances and the situation.

You might have a fixed mindset about money but a growth mindset when it comes to relationships. It can vary, or it can be a mix of the two. If you say that you are complaining, the more important part is that your complaints are reduced. Waiting for a condition where you have zero complaints, an ideal situation, is something that may not be practically possible.

Being human, we all face situations where there will be complaints, no matter how much we have worked on ourselves. What is more important is to march towards a growth mindset. Pay attention to which area of your life you have a fixed mindset for and for which one you think about growth. The area that lacks a growth mindset needs more of your attention. Work on it to change it. Other areas are still good, and you might not need any change in your mindset for them. That is how it may vary.

Think of a person who has grown his business from rags to riches. You would say that since he changed his beliefs and brought success to his business, he has a growth mindset. But the same person fights at home every day, unable to maintain a healthy relationship. What would you say about his mindset then?

One person who has been able to change his beliefs about business is unable to change them for his relationships. Like him, no one is perfect, and we all need to work on our mindsets.

I will tell you how I try to remember this in my life so that you can benefit from my theories.

The Law of Dominating Mindset

This is where I want to introduce the **Law of Dominant Mindset** or **LDM.** It is not about having only a growth mindset or only a fixed mindset because we will always have both. It is about noticing which mindset is dominant in your thoughts.

At any point, either your **growth mindset** or your **fixed mindset** is driving your behaviour.

That dominant mindset decides how you think, feel, act and what results you create.

Here are some signs which tell you that your fixed mindset is dominating:

'This is just how I am . . . I can't change.'
'If they're successful, they must have something special . . . I don't have it.'
'My luck is always bad.'
'Everything looks negative to me.'
'I can never be that smart.'
'I can't do this . . . I should just give up.'

And when your growth mindset becomes dominant, your thoughts sound very different:

'I can learn this if I try.'
'Failures teach me something valuable.'
'If others can do it, I can figure it out too.'
'Setbacks are temporary, not permanent.'
'Let me improve 1 per cent every day.'
'I may not know it yet, but I will.'

When you analyse yourself, you may notice a contrast. For example, in money, your thoughts are mostly fearful, doubtful and blaming (fixed mindset is dominant). And in relationships, you are open, hopeful and willing to improve (growth mindset is dominant)

This contrast shows you **which mindset is dominant in which area.**

Remember, we are not trying to instantly jump from a fixed mindset to a growth mindset. We are simply walking the journey, step by step. And as your **dominant mindset** shifts, you will see changes not just in your results but in your happiness, joy, relationships, peace and your sense of who you are.

You don't have to become perfect. You only need to keep changing what dominates your mind. That alone will change your life.

How Our Mindset Works

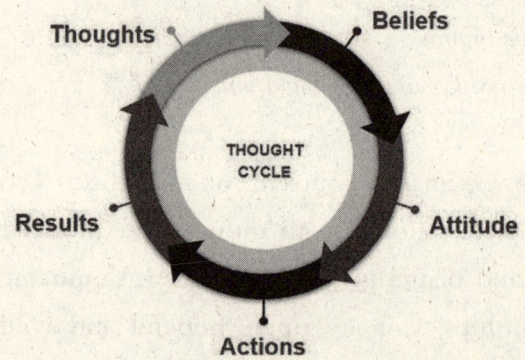

Your thoughts make your belief, your beliefs, build your attitude, your attitude decides your action, your action gives you results and your results decide your further thoughts.

That is why it is a cycle, a loop, and not a unidirectional movement. When you change your thoughts, they keep changing the entire cycle. All words will move in the direction you choose, positive and progressive or negative and depressing.

Suppose a person finds it difficult to run a business. His thought process is that he is not meant for business, so he can never be successful. When it becomes his belief, he comes across all the negative examples of business, of failure, and he keeps getting convinced that he was right about his belief. Because of this attitude, he would not do anything about it. Even if he does, it would be a wrong decision. That would impact the results negatively, again forming negative thoughts about it and making his belief stronger that he is not meant for business. He will eventually give up or become a failure in business.

Your thoughts become your core belief, and it all comes down to your mindset and your belief keeps contributing to the thought cycle.

A person who is bullied when trying out public speaking for the first time would develop a belief that speaking up makes you a target for others. With this attitude, he stops speaking up and suffers silently. Every time he got a chance to speak after that would make him nervous and give negative results, making his belief stronger and growing up into a nervous adult.

Managing the Thought Factory

I would like to share an analogy: think of your mind as a **factory that produces different types of thoughts.** This factory has two departments: the **Fixed Department** and the **Growth Department.** Each department has an obedient department head working for you: **Udaas Singh** (Fixed) and **Happy Singh** (Growth). They both follow your commands faithfully.

If your dominant mindset is fixed, it means **Udaas Singh occupies more space in your factory**, and most of the production happens in his department, leaving little space for **Happy Singh** to manufacture positive thoughts.

Imagine waking up early in the morning and having an argument at home. The next statement that slips out is, *'It's going to be a bad day.'*

When this command reaches **Udaas Singh**, your fixed mindset, he immediately salutes and says, *'Yes sir,* *as you say.*' Now you're more irritated in the same traffic, more stressed with the same workload, more frustrated with the same boss—and this spiral keeps worsening your day. By the time you return home, you're in a terrible mood, which leads to yet another argument.

At the end of the day, you're convinced that the **morning argument caused the bad day**, but in reality, it was **your command to Udaas Singh** that shaped everything.

Think about it: every time you've believed your day wouldn't go well, it usually hasn't because your mind followed your command.

The same thing happens when you're about to take a risk or step out of your comfort zone. If the fixed mindset is dominant, **Udaas Singh will stop you.** He'll convince you it's beyond your capacity, remind you of your past failures and point to others who failed at similar attempts. Slowly, your confidence collapses, and the fixed mindset grows even stronger.

That's why the only thing you truly need to focus on is **keeping Happy Singh active—consciously.**

Once you do that, the entire cycle shifts: your thoughts change your beliefs, your beliefs shape your attitude, your attitude drives your actions and your actions transform your results—almost on autopilot.

That is the power of every single thought you choose.

In the next chapter, I'll walk you through the **Seven Fundamentals of a Growth Mindset**—seven powerful shifts that will make Happy Singh stronger every day. These fundamentals will help you break your inner limits, build unstoppable confidence and move through life with clarity and courage. Once you master these fundamentals, you won't have to fight a fixed mindset each time. A growth mindset will automatically take the lead, like an invisible current pulling you forward.

Conclusion

Your skills, degrees, and even your talent can take you far, but your mindset decides whether you'll start, sustain and succeed. It's the invisible steering wheel behind every visible achievement.

So, before you look outward for solutions, pause and look within. Ask yourself: which mindset is driving you right now? Is it the voice that says, *'I can't,'* or the one that whispers, *'I can figure it out'*?

Because once you change the driver, the journey changes.

Once you choose the growth mindset as your dominant force, everything begins to expand—your ideas, your courage, your results, your joy.

Remember: **your mindset doesn't just shape your life; it drives it.**

//
Chapter 4

Seven Fundamentals of Growth Mindset

Two years ago, something interesting happened that completely shifted how I look at challenges.

Within the same week, I had two very different conversations—one with someone who leads a massive empire, and another with someone who was just beginning to build theirs.

The first was a founder I invited to my podcast—he manages over 5000 people across multiple companies. While we were chatting off-camera, I asked him something: 'Handling large-scale projects and juggling between different verticals . . . It sometimes feels overwhelming. How do you manage operations at this scale?'

He smiled and said, 'Oh, that's not really a problem. Let me show you how we handle it,' and in just ten minutes, he broke it down with such clarity that it felt surprisingly simple.

A few days later, I met a rising influencer who had just crossed a million followers on Instagram and was doing well with his coaching business. While we spoke, he looked at me and asked, almost in disbelief, 'How are you able to create so much content, manage a team, get the production and editing done, and keep up with all your platforms?'

I smiled back and said almost the same words I'd heard earlier that week: 'Oh, that's not really a problem. Let me help you out.'

That's when it struck me: **The same thing that felt heavy for me was light for someone ahead of me. And the same thing that felt heavy for him was light for me.**

Imagine a weighing scale. On one side, you place your **problems**. On the other side, you place your **mental strength**.

If your mental strength is light and your problem is heavy, the scale tilts and the problem dominates you. But if your mental strength becomes heavier than the problem, the scale shifts in your favour.

The weight of the problem hasn't changed, you just became stronger.

This is the truth most people miss: Successful people didn't make their problems smaller. They simply kept adding more weight—**more skills, more resilience, more clarity, more belief**—onto the side of their mental strength.

The goal isn't to keep removing problems from your life. The goal is to **load up your side of the scale** until no problem feels heavy anymore.

And that's exactly what the **Seven Fundamentals of a Growth Mindset** will help you do. Each fundamental you learn will act like an extra weight placed on your side of the scale. One by one, they'll make your mind stronger, heavier and steadier . . . Until your problems stop shaking you and start shaping you.

Seven Fundamentals of a Growth Mindset

Consider these fundamentals as your road map to a more empowered, fulfilling life. Dive in wholeheartedly and watch as your mindset evolves, unlocking doors that you never thought existed. These are the transformative principles that hold the power to unlock your true potential. By embracing them, you'll cultivate a mindset brimming with positivity and the resilience to turn every challenge into a golden opportunity.

Let's start this journey to greatness!

1. Taking responsibility

Our mind is an extraordinary machine but sometimes, it works against our own growth.

Whenever we fail to do something, our brain immediately begins its search for reasons why we failed. Not solutions, but reasons. It works hard to protect our ego, to comfort us and to make us feel safe. But in doing so, it quietly turns us into victims.

If we are late, we blame the traffic. If we don't succeed, we blame our family conditions, our past, our education, our colleagues, our boss, our company, even our country. Our mind whispers, '*It's not your fault.*'

And for a brief moment, that thought feels comforting. It gives us a safe zone. But that comfort comes with a hidden cost—it silently steals our power. Because when the mind convinces you that others are responsible for where you are, it also convinces you that you can't change it. The power, it says, belongs to your situation, not to you.

Interestingly, notice how we never complain about things we can't change. No one wakes up frustrated at gravity, even though gravity makes things break, makes us fall and causes accidents. Instead, we accept it and even use it to our advantage to build drainage systems, amusement park rides, swings. Why? Because we know it cannot be changed.

But when something *can* be changed and we don't change it, our mind begins creating excuses. It gives us the illusion of safety, but it quietly stops our growth.

Look around and you'll see this everywhere.

Two children grow up in the same house, under the same conditions. One says, 'I couldn't succeed because my father was poor.' The other says, 'I succeeded because I refused to let poverty define me.' One son becomes an addict, 'My father was always on drugs, so I became like him.' The other never touches drugs and says, 'I saw my father every day, and I decided I would not repeat that story.'

Same conditions. Same environment. Same childhood. Yet two completely different outcomes because **one found excuses and the other took responsibility.**

Growth has never come from excuses. **Every person who has grown has done it by choosing responsibility over excuses.**

And this is where the real shift begins. Because once you stop giving your power to the trigger and start owning your response, you stop being a victim and start becoming the author of your future.

Future = Trigger + Response

Whatever future you experience, it is a result of your responses to triggers that have occurred in your life. How happy or sad, rich or poor, confident or underconfident you are, is all the output of how you responded to a certain incident or occurrence.

Imagine this: You apply for your dream job. You've worked hard, gone through multiple rounds and you can already see yourself there. And then, the email comes: *'We regret to inform you . . .'*

That rejection becomes the **Trigger (T).**

Now, what happens next depends entirely on your **Response (R).**

One person might take it personally, assume they're not good enough, stop applying and slowly lose confidence. Another person might treat the same rejection as feedback. They'll reflect, upgrade their skills, prepare better and apply again with more clarity and energy.

Here's the interesting part: **The trigger was the same, but their futures won't be.**

For the first person, the future becomes smaller. For the second person, the same rejection becomes the launchpad to something even better.

Similarly, you watch an advertisement of a smoking hot pizza. Instantly, you have a craving. It is an event. How you respond to it is going to decide the output. Suppose you didn't give in to your craving; the output is your controlled weight.

That's the power of $F = T + R$. Your future isn't shaped by what happens to you, but by how you respond to what happens.

Now you can relate this equation to various events in your life and examine when you took action and when you didn't. Reflecting on those events or incidents, you can look at the output with a new perspective.

At the recent Olympics, Annu Rani was a player in Javelin throw. Initially, she didn't have any money to buy a javelin, so she used to practise with sugarcane sticks. Her response to the lack of resources was practice and the output was her participation in Olympics.

Hence, it is not resource that matters, it is resourcefulness.

We keep complaining all our life about our house, family, job, money, place, city and everything around us. However, it is not about the resources you had or did not have, but about how resourceful you have been. Even if you don't have anything, if you are resourceful enough, you will succeed. Whatever output you receive will depend on how you respond to a particular trigger.

Replace Complaints with Responsibilities

I had a word with a company CEO once who was complaining that despite explaining the same thing over and over again, his team leaders weren't able to understand anything at all.

I asked him one thing. 'If they don't understand what you are telling them, how many ways have *you* used to make them understand?'

If you keep complaining without trying to find a solution, it is an indication of a fixed mindset. But trying different ways to achieve your goal if one way is not working is taking ownership and showing determination.

Excuses are walls where you keep banging your head, finding no solution or a way to move forward.

There could be limitations of resources or capabilities, but having a growth mindset would help you find ways to move forward and achieve your dreams, no matter how big or small they are.

> *Mirror Moment: List some of your common complaints, and against each, note one way you can take responsibility. For instance: 'I don't have time' → 'I'll plan my each day and block priorities.'*

Complaints	Responsibility

2. Empowering Words

If I ask you to think about a forest, what is the first thing that comes to your mind? Your most probable answers will be trees, bushes and wild animals, but not the word F-O-R-E-S-T.

Similarly, if I ask you to think about shoes, you will visualize actual shoes, sneakers, formal shoes, running shoes, different brands or colours of shoes, but not the word S-H-O-E-S.

One never thinks about the word, but visualizes the meaning or feels the emotion instantly. What we often forget is that every word carries its own emotional charge and visual. Each word is like a seed—you plant it in your mind every time you speak it.

Yet we use words casually, as if they are harmless. We keep repeating words that quietly strengthen our fixed mindset. When you say, 'I'm such a **failure**,' it labels your identity. But when you say, 'I'm still **learning**,' it labels the phase as temporary. Saying 'life is unfair' creates hopelessness, while saying 'life is helping me grow' sparks resilience. 'I can't' shuts your mind down, while 'I can' opens it up.

Every word you speak is a command to your brain. With every word, you are either building castles or digging graves—brick by brick, thought by thought.

When I became aware of this fact, I noticed that people with a growth mindset are very careful about the words they choose to speak. They don't want to push their life into chaos and negativity by thinking badly about anything. Since they focus on their growth and aim to move forward, *they look before they leap.* They are always careful about the words they choose.

What comes to your mind when you think of the word 'problem'?

A common impression of a problem is loss, a negative image. If you are unable to think positively, and only negative images come to your mind about problems, then why not change your words?

Think of your childhood when you used to get challenges. How happily you would find a solution and glow with pride. This is exactly how you need to work on your 'problem'.

Why not to call your problem a 'challenge' instead?

Do it, put it in practice and feel the change. You will find yourself thinking about solutions. Solve it and grow with each challenge.

Instead of saying, 'I can't do this,' try saying, 'I haven't figured it out yet.' Instead of saying, 'This is too hard,' try saying, 'This is new for me.'

Growth minded people know that they have to keep their energy high and it is purely their responsibility. So, they are always careful about the words they speak

Mirror Moment: List all the mindless or negative words you use in your daily life and replace them with mindful or positive words.

Fixed Mindset Words	Growth Mindset Words

3. Admire and Inspire

There is an emotion that is naturally evoked in our lives at every possible opportunity. It makes Udaas Singh do a lot of work and puts Happy Singh aside.

It occurs whenever someone around you grows. For instance, your neighbour bought a new car, your relative shifted to a bigger house, your friend's son scored better than your child or someone got promoted in your office.

Yes, you got it right! It is 'jealousy'. Jealousy is a feeling that many times creates a problem in you, bringing negative energy with it. This insecurity, this bad feeling, is detrimental.

There was a time when jealousy quietly slipped into my journey.

Back in 2017, I was creating content in the personal development space—motivational videos, mindset lessons, tools for self-growth. For years, I had been consistently building my audience, slowly climbing the ladder one step at a time.

Then, in just a matter of months, I saw two or three new creators enter the same space. Their growth was explosive. They reached those same milestones in two years that had taken me much longer. One of them even crossed me—more views, more engagement, more subscribers.

I wish I could say I clapped for them, but the truth is, I didn't. I felt jealous. I was restless, frustrated, even angry. My inner voice kept saying, *'How can he cross me? I've worked so hard for so long. I can't let this happen.'*

But jealousy is like a slow poison. It clouds your thinking. It pulls your focus from creation to competition.

It doesn't let you celebrate others, and it doesn't let you create your best work either.

During that phase, through my own self-work and reading, I stumbled upon a realization that changed everything:

You cannot create positive results from a negative state of mind. You cannot grow with jealousy in your heart.

Because think about it: If I feel threatened when someone works hard, what emotion am I attaching to hard work? If I resent someone's growth, what emotion am I attaching to growth itself? If I dislike someone's achievement, what signal am I sending to my own mind about achievement?

I realized something profound: **If you carry negative emotions toward success, happiness and growth, you will unconsciously push them away from your own life.**

So, I made a decision. Instead of being jealous, I would be **inspired**. Instead of competing in anger, I would **admire and learn.** And everything changed.

The moment I started seeing other creators' growth as proof that more is possible, my own ideas became sharper. My energy became positive again. I worked more consistently. I grew faster. I felt lighter.

I often tell people: If you want a better house, but you feel jealousy toward people living in better houses, how will you ever attract one? If you want a happy family, but you feel resentment toward people who have one, how will you create that joy in your own home? If you want success, but you secretly dislike those who succeed, how can you ever walk toward what you secretly despise?

Jealousy closes doors. Admiration opens them. When you replace jealousy with admiration, every successful person becomes your teacher. And your heart becomes free to grow again.

I have worked on it a lot. I have changed such feelings to admiration, appreciation, praise and compliment. You can do it too. It is not going to be an overnight change, but practice and conscious efforts can make it happen.

4. Appreciate

You go to a restaurant. There is a problem with the food. You will call the staff immediately to complain about it and replace it. But do you appreciate it if you find it tasty?

Out of fifty times that you had good food at the restaurant, there was one time when it was not up to the mark. You immediately take action and complain, but never appreciate any of those forty-nine times when the food was remarkably good.

One of the simplest and most powerful ways to develop a growth mindset is to **build the habit of appreciation**. For instance, during my travels, whenever I check out of any hotel, I write an honest compliment about property, staff or service on the notepad in the room and wish them well.

If we pay attention, there is always something to appreciate. The hotel and its staff might get a lot of direct or indirect benefits from my appreciation. My focus is to activate my Happy Singh and keep him working.

When you consciously look for what's good in people, situations and even in yourself, you train your mind to focus on the positive. Every time you appreciate something, you're essentially telling your mind, *'Find more of this'*. Slowly, this rewires your brain to become opportunity-oriented instead of problem-obsessed.

Here's the magic: If you consistently practise appreciation, then when a challenge appears, your first instinct won't be panic, it will be curiosity. Instead of thinking *'Why is this happening to me?'*, you will naturally think, *'What can I learn from this?'* You begin to see obstacles as lessons, not punishments.

People who appreciate are often happier too, because they spend more time noticing their blessings than counting their burdens. They see the good they have, not just what's missing. And this isn't about ignoring reality or pretending everything is perfect; it's about keeping your focus on what empowers you to move forward.

Also, appreciation strengthens your voice. If you are someone who regularly appreciates others, then when you do have a complaint or need to give negative feedback, people listen. They know your words are balanced and sincere. But if you only complain and never appreciate, your words slowly lose their impact.

So, acknowledge small efforts. Say thank you more than you think is necessary. **The more you appreciate, the more your mind learns to see the good and the more naturally your growth mindset activates.**

> *Mirror Moment: Write down **five things you genuinely appreciate in your life right now.** They can be small or big—a person, an opportunity, your health, a quality in yourself, something that went well today . . . anything.*
>
> -
> -
> -
> -
> -

It shows that all of us have uncountable blessings in our life, but our focus is only on sufferings that are negligible.

5. Acceptance

A few years ago, I planned a big surprise for a friend's birthday. I gathered people, arranged decorations, got a personalized gift and made the entire evening special. A few months later, when my birthday came, the same friend sent me a heartfelt message and brought a small cupcake.

It was kind, but a part of me felt disappointed. My mind instantly compared: 'I did ten things, and they just brought one cupcake?' But then I realized this is how they express care. For me, celebration meant effort, planning and scale. For them, celebration meant thoughtfulness and presence.

The intention was there, just wrapped differently. And once I saw that, I could feel grateful instead of hurt.

We often expect others to love, care or support us the way we love, care or support them. Now I've stopped measuring people by how closely their way of showing care matches mine.

I often remind myself:

> 'If our fingerprints, retinas and faces are all different, how can our ways of expressing love, care and relationships be identical?'

This simple mindset shift has protected many of my relationships and, more importantly, brought me peace.

Accept People

Every person is different. I present flowers to my wife because I know that she likes it. This is my way of showing affection. She cares for me in her own ways, looking after my health and fitness requirements since she knows that I don't pay much attention to my diet schedules.

If I start questioning her ways, I would do nothing but lose her admiration. Instead, we bask in the beauty of our bond.

If you observe closely, you'll notice a simple pattern in life: People who carry higher expectations often carry higher stress.

We expect our family members to behave a certain way. We expect our friend to reply to our messages on time. We expect our colleagues to speak in the tone we like. We even expect strangers to treat us according to our invisible rules.

We get irritated when someone doesn't call back. We feel disrespected because a salesperson didn't give us attention. We get frustrated because someone didn't turn off the light or left the towel on the bed. We even feel annoyed at our neighbour for painting his house a colour we don't like.

We even carry expectations into places where we have zero control. While watching a cricket match, we scream, 'Why did he bowl like that!' While driving, we yell inside our cars at strangers who can't hear us. They don't even know they've caused us stress but we're boiling from inside.

Now, this doesn't mean you must accept everything silently. Acceptance is not passivity; it's clarity.

There's a difference between:

- **Expecting in your mind and getting stressed**, and
- **Accepting their nature first, and then calmly communicating.**

If you want your partner to spend more quality time with you, you can either keep expecting it and feel hurt when it doesn't happen, **or** you can express your need gently and plan specific time together.

If you want your friend to return your calls, you can either keep expecting it and feel ignored every time they don't, **or** you can simply tell them how much it matters to you and ask if there's a better time to connect.

If you're angry at how people drive, screaming alone in your car won't change anything. But if you really want change, start spreading awareness. Maybe create a campaign or make short videos to educate others.

Remember, with the burden of expectations, your only achievement is to disturb your own mindset and get stuck. If you keep expecting from others without taking appropriate action yourself, the result is always going to be disappointing.

Knowing that such things cause sadness and disappointment, what is the use of holding onto them? Your findings through the '5 Whys' exercise say that your goal is only one: happiness. Then,

- Why not drop expectations and work towards your goal?
- Why not choose happiness purposefully?
- Why not free your mind from the weight of control and give yourself the space to feel light, peaceful and happy?

This a simple philosophy. If something is not keeping you happy, there is no point in keeping it around you. The same thing applies to your expectations as well.

Accept Change

A married couple fails to understand that nothing is going to remain the same in the following years—body, looks, intimacy, everything. Where physical intimacy plays a vital role in the beginning, emotional support means a lot more in the later part of the marriage, with a lot of more responsibilities and added engagement with jobs, children and careers coming in. Not realizing this, couples keep expecting the same first year behaviour from their partners and get disappointed by their relationship. Even a marriage goes through different stages.

Similarly, parents feel disheartened at their grown-up children's behaviour, without accepting that their children have developed their own minds and perspectives.

People with older parents fail to accept that old age has brought in a lot of insecurities as well as fragile and sensitive bodies, and keep expecting the same from their parents, resulting in frustration and arguments.

Focusing on all these expectations makes us stray from our goals, clarity and growth.

Accept Mental Wounds

During a corporate workshop, I noticed an employee engaged with his phone despite my repeated reminders to take notes. When it became too much, I confronted him, only to realize that he was taking notes on his mobile.

In another such instance, I had a team member who suddenly started performing poorly. It frustrated me a lot, troubling him more in return, but I did not talk to him about it openly. A few days later, I came to know that he had been going through divorce.

Had I talked to him, I would have a clear idea about his poor mental health. It would have helped me understand him and his situation better.

Imagine this: You're walking in your office and you accidentally crash into a table. You're hurt, bleeding or in visible pain. Immediately, everyone around you rushes to help. Someone brings water, someone checks if you're okay, someone calls for first aid.

Why? Because physical wounds are visible. We are used to them. We understand how to respond to them. So, we show care.

But what we often forget is: **People carry mental wounds too and those are invisible.**

Everyone you meet has a past. Everyone has their share of fears, insecurities and emotional scars. Some wounds come from childhood. Some from yesterday.

Yet, because they are invisible, we forget they exist. We assume that if someone *looks fine*, they *are* fine—and that's rarely true. When you remember this, it changes how you see people.

If a friend seems obsessed with saving money, maybe it's not greed—maybe it's the fear from growing up in poverty. If a colleague appears rude or guarded, maybe they carry the wounds of being betrayed before. If someone struggles to trust you, maybe they were deeply hurt when they trusted someone else.

Accepting mental wounds doesn't mean tolerating every behaviour. It simply means pausing before judging and asking, *'Could there be pain I can't see?'*

Because just like physical wounds need bandages, **mental wounds need understanding.** And when you learn to accept the wounds you cannot see, you become far better at accepting the people who carry them.

A fixed mindset is quick to judge: it labels people as lazy, careless, arrogant or weak based only on what's visible on the surface. But a growth mindset looks deeper. It asks, *'What might this person be carrying that I can't see?'*

Mirror Moment: Take a moment and write down the names of **three people** *whose behaviour has recently irritated, disappointed or hurt you. Next to each name, answer this question honestly. Could this person be carrying a wound I cannot see? (Fear, insecurity, rejection, betrayal, loneliness, failure, loss . . .)*

_____

_____

_____

6. Managing Emotions

Aman Sehrawat was only eleven years old when he lost both his parents. He was devastated and always angry. Instead of reacting to his situation, he channelled all his emotions into wrestling and brought his country glory by winning a bronze medal at the 2024 Paris Olympics, at the age of twenty-one. Not only that, his determination and success made him the youngest Indian to win an Olympic Medal. Similar was the case of superstar Shah Rukh Khan when he lost his parents. He worked so hard that we all know the position he has acquired in the film industry for decades.

*What comes out in anger is a **reaction**; what you do after thinking is a **response**.*

Don't react, respond to emotions.

Let me share an experience. I was eleven years old when I witnessed a lesson that stayed with me for life.

We were travelling together as a family—my father driving, my mother beside him and my brother and I in the back seat. My father was a strong Punjabi man, the kind whose presence alone could silence a noisy room, almost like Sunny Deol from the movie *Gadar*.

While we were driving on a quiet road, out of nowhere, a tractor rammed into our car from behind.

Before we could even process what had happened, it hit us again. And again.

My mother gasped in shock. My brother and I were frightened. Anger bubbled up instantly: 'Who is this guy? What's he doing?!'

My father, however, stayed completely calm. He first looked at my mother and at both of us, and asked one simple question: 'Are you all okay?'

We nodded. We were all perfectly fine, not a scratch on us.

Then my father slowed the car, pushed the side mirror down and let the tractor driver pull up next to us. The man driving the tractor was visibly nervous, almost trembling. He probably thought my father was going to step out and shout at him.

Instead, my father leaned slightly out of the window and gently asked, 'Are you okay?'

The tractor driver, stunned, nodded and said softly, 'Yes, saab.'

'Good,' my father replied. 'Drive safely. Take care.'

And then we simply drove away.

I remember asking him, almost confused, 'Weren't you angry? The car must be damaged from the back.'

He smiled and said something that etched itself into my heart forever:

'The car is already damaged. Now should I damage my health too? Should I ruin our evening and family time as well?'

That day, my father taught me the power of choosing a response over giving a reaction.

Your emotional management helps you in making friends, establishing relations and strengthening bonds, whereas an emotional reaction will do nothing but harm you, your relations and any possibilities of good occurrences in the future.

If you wish to make your growth mindset dominant, hold the keys of your happiness in your hands by responding. Don't hand them over to others by reacting.

7. Practise Gratitude

Every morning, I practise gratitude. Even being thankful for the incident that took place on 6 December 1999. I was shaped into the person I am today because of the struggles my family faced for the next ten years after that particular date.

Had it been any normal day, I would have been the spoiled brat of a wealthy father. I wouldn't be taking sessions. I wouldn't be receiving so much love and blessings from my 11 million subscribers and followers across social media.

I thank life for the love I receive, the lives I get to impact, the team I'm able to guide, the family that surrounds me, the health I've been given and even for something as simple yet miraculous as being able to breathe, see, hear, walk and move.

This practice might sound simple, but it is powerful.

Our minds are naturally wired to look for what's wrong—to scan for risks, threats and missing pieces. It's a survival instinct that often fuels a fixed mindset. We become so busy noticing what's lacking that we forget to notice what's already abundant.

But when you practise gratitude, you flip that switch.

If you pause for a moment and reflect, you will realize how much you already have. If you can eat three meals a day, if you have a roof over your head, if you have even one person who cares about you—you are already richer than millions. If your body allows you to move, see or speak with ease, that alone is a silent blessing we often overlook.

Gratitude gently reminds you that **life has already given you so much to stand on. Now it's your turn to rise.**

I can say from experience: every morning when I practise gratitude, something changes inside me. My energy rises. My mind becomes solution-oriented instead of problem-focused. I feel calmer, clearer and more confident. It's as if a light switches on inside me that says, *'You are blessed. You are ready. Go and make this day count.'*

Shift Expectations to Gratitude

Gratitude, or thankfulness, is a job for Happy Singh. It is a simple act, but it can transform how you experience life. Every time you appreciate what you have, you give Happy Singh a chance to shine.

Do you let Happy Singh acknowledge their efforts? Or do you let negativity creep in, remembering only the times they couldn't show up?

There is so much to be grateful for on a smaller and larger scale throughout your life. If you are conscious enough, you will be able to recognize and acknowledge them.

When you let Happy Singh do his work, these moments become treasures. When you don't, you miss the beauty of what's right in front of you.

> **Gratitude doesn't require a lot of time, instead it requires an appreciation of what you have got.**
>
> *Mirror Moment: Write down **5 things you are grateful for today or in life**. They can be small (your morning tea, your laptop, mobile) or big (your health, family, work, opportunities). Next to each, write **why** you're grateful for it.*
>
> _____
>
> _____
>
> _____
>
> _____
>
> _____

Each time you acknowledge these things, you fuel your mind with positivity. On the days when life feels heavy and the going gets tough, these notes can serve as gentle reminders of the good things you've experienced. Life will never be perfect, but when you focus on what's good—family, friends and little joys—you allow Happy Singh to work his magic, brightening your days.

Conclusion

When you begin to embrace the 'Seven Fundamentals of a Growth Mindset', you unlock a world of endless possibilities. It starts with **taking responsibility**—owning your actions, your thoughts and your emotions. No one else can drive your growth; it's in your hands. Follow it up with **using empowering words**. The language you speak to yourself and others shapes your reality. Positive words create a positive mindset, propelling you forward.

Admire and get inspired by those who have walked the path before you. Don't see their success as a threat, but as proof that growth is possible. **When you accept** people, change and even hidden wounds, you stop resisting life and start growing with it..

Appreciation trains your mind to spot the good, even inside challenges. **Mastering your emotions** means choosing responses that build, not reactions that break and **gratitude** is the switch that turns on your growth mindset each day.

Remember, growth isn't a destination. It's a journey. By practising these fundamentals every day, you shape your future, one empowered choice at a time.

Take charge of your life and let the world watch as you transform into the best version of yourself!

Chapter 5

From Confusion to Clarity

In almost every seminar I conduct, I love asking a simple question to the audience: 'What are the ten things you want in your life?'

Then I randomly pick someone and hand them the mic.

What happens next is always the same—they pause, smile awkwardly and start thinking. After a few seconds, they manage to mention one thing. Then another. Then they fall silent again, trying hard to think of a third.

And while they struggle, I notice something magical happening. The entire hall, hundreds of people, also begin silently thinking, 'Wait . . . what do I want in my life?'

And here's the shocking part: I've been asking this question for years, and not even once has someone confidently stood up and listed ten things they want. Rarely do I hear five. Most people realize, in that very moment, that they've never truly thought about it before.

We study, work, chase deadlines, earn money and keep running every day but if you pause and ask *why* you are doing it all, most people don't have a clear answer.

It's like walking up to an airport ticket counter and saying, 'Excuse me, I want a ticket.'

The staff member will ask, 'Sure ... but where do you want to go?'

And you say, 'I don't know.'

No airline, no pilot, no rocket in the world can take you somewhere if **you don't know where you want to go.**

Your life works the same way. If you don't know what you want, your mind can't focus. Your brain can't align. Your subconscious can't support you. Even the best people and the best opportunities around you won't know how to help you.

But the moment you become clear about what you want, something incredible happens. Your energy starts aligning. Your focus sharpens. Ideas begin to appear. People start showing up who can help you. And resources begin falling into place like puzzle pieces.

That's why I always say:

If you don't know what you want from life, you will always get what you 'don't' want in life.

Since you would never like to have just 'anything', you should know very well what you want and wish to achieve.

Let's have a kick-start of clarity.

I know there are confusions and doubts. I don't say that you will be sure of everything right away, but you will begin to understand. Over the period, you will have an absolute clarity of what you want from life. This will happen if you are able to sort your thoughts, and that is what I am going to guide you with.

Before we begin, a quick note. What you're about to do will take time and effort—you'll have to pause, reflect and spend honest moments with yourself, but it's worth it.

This is not just an activity; it's an investment that can save you years of confusion and regret, and give you clarity that can transform your life.

So yes, I'm going to make you work, and trust me, it will be one of the best investments you'll ever make in yourself.

Are You Chasing the Right Goals?

Sometimes, in a burst of enthusiasm, we set goals without fully understanding what we truly want. Maybe you walked out of a powerful movie, completely inspired by the acts of its hero, and decided, *This is it! This is my life's purpose!*

Or you watched a motivational video, set an ambitious goal and even achieved it; only to feel strangely empty afterward. It never brought you the satisfaction or happiness you were looking for.

Does this sound familiar? You're not alone.

After speaking with countless individuals in personal sessions, I've realized a common pattern—many people chase goals without first understanding themselves.

That's why we talked about **happiness** in the initial chapters. Because at the root of every goal, every dream and every ambition, what we are truly seeking is *fulfilment*.

> *Mirror Moment: The 'Wheel of Life' Test*
>
> *On a scale of 1 to 10, rate yourself in each area of the 'Wheel of Life' based on your own sense of fulfilment—not society's standards or others' expectations, but how you genuinely feel about that area of your life right now, with 10 being the highest and 1 the lowest. After marking your rating, connect all the marked points and draw a circle.*
>
>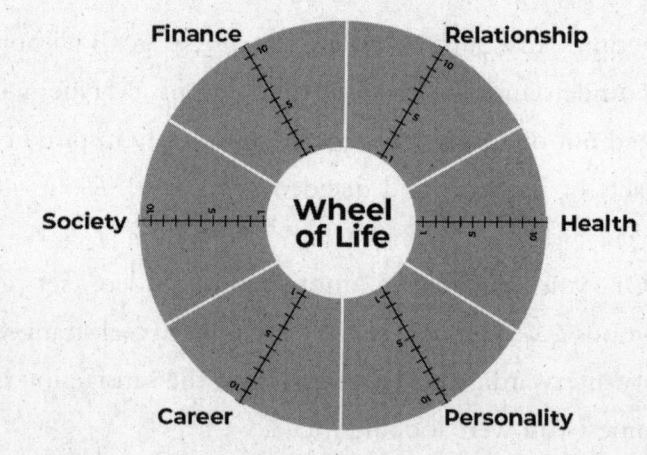

What do you see?

If your wheel is uneven, it means there are areas you need to focus on. A balanced life doesn't mean being perfect in all areas, but it does mean making conscious improvements where needed.

Before setting goals, understand what truly matters to you. Don't chase success blindly; chase fulfilment, and success will follow.

Imagine trying to ride a bike with a bent wheel. No matter how hard you pedal, it's going to be a rough, uncomfortable ride. That's exactly how life feels when one area is flourishing but another is completely ignored.

Let's say you're earning well, but you regret not having time for your family. Or maybe you're super fit, but you are not happy with the fact that your career isn't going anywhere. In both cases, you'll feel something is missing. And that 'something' is balance.

From Confusion to Clarity

Now that you've mapped your Wheel of Life and seen which areas are strong and which need attention, it's time for the real breakthrough.

What you're about to do next is not just another exercise; it's a turning point.

This next part is going to be deeply practical and personal. Through a series of guided questions and activities, I will help you dive into your inner world, so you can: identify what truly matters to you, understand what you really want in life and build a list of aspirations and goals that are yours, and not borrowed from the world around you.

I've watched people experience pure euphoria during this part of my workshops. I've seen participants come back to me years later and say, 'That activity was a rebirth for me. It gave me the clarity I had been searching for all my life.'

This is how powerful clarity can be. It can save you years. It can save you from regret. It can make your life more meaningful, memorable, fulfilling and fill it with happiness.

And if while doing this exercise you still feel unsure or your goals don't feel perfectly clear, that's completely okay. Clarity is not a one-time achievement; it's a journey. Even writing something half-clear is better than leaving the page blank, because a moving compass always finds its direction. You can keep coming back to this exercise as life unfolds. Every revisit will bring deeper understanding and sharper focus. The point is not to get it perfect, but to get it *started*.

Step 1: Build Your Wish List

Look again at your Wheel of Life. You now know which areas you are doing well in, and which areas need more attention.

For each area, ask yourself: *'What would I love to experience, achieve, or improve in this part of my life?'*

Write everything that comes to mind. Don't filter. Don't judge. Don't worry about practicality or logic right now. This is your space to dream.

It could be something as simple as:

- Reading one book every month to grow your wisdom.
- Calling your parents or friends every weekend.
- Getting back to your fitness routine.
- Travelling to a new city every year.
- Saving Rs 10 lakh this year.
- Starting your own business.
- Learning a new language or skill.
- Improving your relationship with your partner.

> *Mirror Moment: Whether you write five things or fifty, it's completely fine. Just let your heart speak.*
> _____
> _____
> _____
> _____
> _____

Step 2: The No-Regret Question

Now, to help your mind go even deeper, I want you to imagine something powerful:

If today was your last day on Earth, what experiences would you wish you had lived? What dreams, if left undone, would make you say, *'I wish I had done that'*? What would make your life feel more complete?

Close your eyes for a moment and think.

Don't worry about how big, difficult, or unrealistic something sounds. This is not about planning; it's about discovering what your heart truly desires.

- That passion project you always wanted to do.
- The country you dreamed of visiting.
- The impact you wanted to create in someone's life.
- The dream business you wanted to start.
- Learning a musical instrument or a dance genre.

> *Mirror Moment: Whatever thoughts come, write them down. Let them flow. We'll sort and refine them later.*
>
> _____
> _____
> _____
> _____
> _____

By this point, most people have at least ten to fifteen things on their list. Some have written forty or fifty. Don't let that overwhelm you; it's a good sign. It means your inner clarity is awakening.

If you need more space, use a separate sheet or page. Right now, the only goal is to capture every spark of desire before it fades.

Step 3: The WHY Filter (Alignment Check)

You now have a living list of wishes, goal, and aspirations. Before you sprint, pause. This is where most people lose years—by chasing things that never truly belonged to them.

Your task now: take every item on your list and run it through the **WHY Filter**. Ask, again and again: **'Why do I want this?'** Use the **5 Whys** you learned earlier—go deeper, third why, fourth why, fifth why—until you reach the root.

Keep it **only if**:

- the WHY **excites** you,
- the WHY feels **yours** (not borrowed from trends, friends, or social media),
- the WHY still makes sense even when things get hard.

If the WHY is weak, vague or driven by validation, **strike it out** or **park it for later**.

How to Run the WHY Filter (Quick Method)

For each goal, write:

'I want because . . .' (answer)

'And why is that important?' (answer)

'And why does that matter to me?' (answer)

Stop when you hit a reason that feels **deep, energizing and undeniably yours**.

Here are some examples which will help you spot the difference:

1. Travel

- *Weak WHY:* 'It looks cool on Instagram.'
- *Strong WHY:* 'I want to experience new cultures, learn humility and feel alive in unfamiliar streets.'

2. Learn Guitar
- *Weak WHY:* 'It's trendy and people will be impressed.'
- *Strong WHY:* 'Music calms me. I want to express myself and play for my family.'"

3. Join the Gym
- *Weak WHY:* 'I need a summer body for photos.'
- *Strong WHY:* 'I want the energy to play with my kids and the stamina to serve my purpose for decades.'

4. Start a Business
- *Weak WHY:* 'I hate my boss.'
- *Strong WHY:* 'There's a problem I care about solving, and I want the freedom to build something meaningful.'

When the WHY is external, your effort dies at the first obstacle. When the WHY is internal, you'll keep going long after the shine wears off.

Imagine a house you must enter. The approach is tough—scorching heat, rough ground, thorny wires, muddy patches, biting insects. Now I tell you there's a **hundred-rupee note** inside. Will you go through all that for a hundred rupees? Probably not.

Now imagine the **person you love most** is inside, calling your name. Would you cross the same path? **Of course.** Same obstacles. Different WHY. Different you.

That is the power of a strong WHY: it doesn't remove the hard parts; it makes you **willing** to face them. Most people quit not because the path is impossible, but because their WHY is too small.

Step 4: The Alignment Filter
(*Find what truly belongs to you*)

You've done the work. You started with your **Wheel of Life**, built a list of **dreams, wishes and goals**, and passed them through the **WHY Filter** to remove the ones driven by trends, comparison or external validation.

Now, it's time for the **final filter**—the one that makes sure what remains on your list is not only clear, but **aligned with who you are and who you want to become.**

This is the **Alignment Filter.**

For every item still on your list, ask yourself these three questions:

The Three Alignment Questions

1. Does it energize me when I imagine it?

Close your eyes and picture yourself living that goal. Does it light you up? Or does it just *sound good* on paper? True dreams feel like fuel, not pressure. If just imagining it drains you, it may not be your dream—it might be someone else's expectation.

2. Am I willing to become the person who can receive this?

Every goal demands growth. If you want to build a business, are you willing to become more disciplined, resilient and courageous? If you want deep love, are you willing to be more patient, honest and vulnerable? If your answer is no, it's just a wish, not a commitment.

3. Would I still want this if no one ever praised me for it?

Imagine achieving it quietly. No applause, no Instagram post, no recognition—just you, silently living it. Would you still want it? This question strips away ego and shows what truly matters to *your soul*, not your image.

These three questions ensure you plant only the seeds that: excite your heart, stretch your character and matter even when no one is watching.

Because **alignment creates consistency** and consistency is what turns dreams into reality.

Congratulations! You've just done something that most people never do. You now hold a list of dreams that are truly yours. Not borrowed. Not copied. Not imposed. And the best part? Every single thing you've written can become real.

In the coming chapters, I'll show you how to build belief around them and bring them to life through manifestation. **Clarity is just the beginning.**

Why This Exercise Matters

This exercise is more than just writing down thoughts. It's about defining your purpose, understanding your values and shaping your future. When you take the time to outline your happiness and aspirations, you create a personal road map that guides you towards a life of fulfilment and success.

1. Clarity Leads to Purpose

When you put your dreams, desires and goals into words, they become more than just passing thoughts. They transform into something real, something you can work towards. Clarity eliminates confusion and helps you focus on what truly matters, preventing you from chasing things that don't align with your deeper purpose.

2. Decision-Making Becomes Easier

Life presents countless choices every day. When you have a clear vision of your ideal life, making decisions becomes effortless. You can ask yourself:

Does this opportunity align with my aspirations? Will this choice bring me closer to my happiness?

Is this investment of time and energy in sync with my ultimate goals?

With this awareness, you won't be easily distracted by things that don't serve your growth.

3. Goals Become More Meaningful

Setting goals without a clear purpose can feel like chasing random targets. But when your goals stem from your personal story, your vision for happiness and success become powerful. You are no longer just working towards something; you are **building your life, one step at a time.**

4. You Stay Motivated Through Challenges

Life is full of ups and downs, but when you have a well-defined vision of what you want, you won't give up easily. Your story serves as a reminder of why you started this journey in the first place. Every challenge becomes a stepping stone rather than an obstacle, pushing you forward instead of holding you back.

5. You Start Living Intentionally

Without a clear vision, it's easy to drift through life, reacting to circumstances rather than creating your own path. But once you define your story, you take control. You become proactive, making choices that align with your happiness, fulfilment and personal growth.

The Calling

This is one thing that you will never see me discussing in my videos because it requires an understanding of all the topics that we explored so far. Since now you have an understanding of your happiness, your core beliefs and fundamentals, we can talk about 'the calling'.

It is not mandatory that you have it, but it is crucial that you know about it. Sometimes, you discover something that justifies your goals and actions in the wheel of life. You get a purpose, a passion that makes you feel fulfilled. Then living a life itself becomes a purpose and you become extraordinary.

Recently, I watched a video of Hollywood actor Arnold Schwarzenegger. He shared that he got a calling for building his body and it became the purpose of his life.

Similarly, when I used to work with airlines, I would find myself talking about life skills during trainings. I could do that due to my experiences and people started liking those bits. It so happened that many lives started to change because of my sharing. As a result, I ventured into life skills training too.

Unfortunately, when I had to watch a nineteen-year-old boy die by suicide in front of me, it gave me the purpose to 'save lives' by spreading an understanding of happiness, life and the importance of having a purpose. I have a mission now and that is the source of my happiness, because I am fulfilling my calling. I work tirelessly.

If you ask me where is my 'work-life balance'? I would say, 'work is my life, so my life is balanced.'

When a person finds their calling, work-life definition has no meaning left for them. They start enjoying every minute of their life spent in serving their purpose. It is not always a big goal. You might not want to be the prime minister of your country, but you might want to make people laugh by becoming a stand-up comedian. You might wish to help in the education of poor children so they can live a better life. You might want to raise your children into good and compassionate human beings for society. It could be anything that gives you the desired level of satisfaction and fulfilment.

Whenever you get your calling, live that mission.

It is the purpose of life. It is something you experience when you shed off a lot of your wishes to fulfil this one.

Conclusion

Clarity is not just about setting goals; it's about creating a road map for your life that aligns with your values and aspirations. It helps you understand your deepest desires, prioritize what truly matters and filter out distractions. Without clarity, you risk being swayed by external influences, chasing goals that don't resonate with your inner self.

When you are clear about your purpose, you begin to see life differently. Decisions become simpler, challenges feel more like stepping stones and the path ahead becomes less daunting. Clarity gives you a sense of direction, helping you stay grounded even amidst uncertainties. It enables you to live with intention, ensuring that every action contributes to your growth and fulfilment.

Moreover, clarity fosters resilience. When setbacks arise, a clear sense of purpose acts as a compass, guiding you back to your path and reigniting your motivation. It also nurtures confidence as knowing what you want allows you to pursue it with conviction and focus.

Ultimately, clarity transforms your life into a meaningful journey. It empowers you to live authentically, achieve your goals with purpose, and find joy in the process. Begin this journey today, and embrace the profound transformation that clarity brings.

The life you envision is closer than you think. All it takes is the courage to seek it!

Chapter 6

The Engine Behind Your Goals

When I started my YouTube channel in 2012, I had to face a lot of negativities. There was hardly a person favouring my vision. The majority of the people gave me nothing but an opinion that pushed me down. All I could hear was:

'YouTube is used only for entertainment.'

'No one is going to watch self-help videos. Data is too expensive.'

But I had a belief that one day, the Internet would become popular, and content around personal growth will become a part of people's life. So, I couldn't be convinced otherwise. With my belief, I kept going on, while people who started in the following years gave up.

Initially I got multiple negative comments related to my looks, communication, video quality, etc. I faced financial setbacks, humiliation and a lot of discouragement. But I kept on building supporting beliefs and strengthening my belief system. I held on to the belief that I would reach masses with my content and build a living around helping people. And it happened. Now, I feel grateful that every day, I get to help people overcome their mental health struggles, manage stress, build confidence, improve their skills, and become happier versions of themselves

The Permission Slip

Clarity gave you a destination. Now your beliefs decide whether you ever leave the driveway.

We've spoken earlier in this book about the power of belief—how your thoughts shape your mindset and your actions. But now, this conversation goes deeper.

Because you've just gained clarity. You've created a list of dreams, wishes and goals that are truly yours. And this is the stage where most people silently fail: **they set big goals, but their inner beliefs are not aligned with them.**

You don't get what you *wish* for; you get what you're **wired** for. If your inner beliefs are out of sync with your new goals, you'll stall, self-sabotage or keep circling the same blocks—no matter how hard you press the accelerator.

Think of belief as the *permission slip* your mind signs before it lets you have something. When the permission is missing, your actions hesitate, your habits wobble and opportunities mysteriously 'don't work out'.

For example, someone may set a goal to build wealth and invest consistently, yet deep inside carry a belief like,

'Money changes people' or 'I'm not good with money'. This inner script quietly creates hesitation: they delay decisions, second-guess themselves, overspend out of guilt or exit too early—and then call it 'bad timing'.

Another person may dream of having a loving and stable relationship, but beneath the surface believe, 'Love always ends in pain' or 'People can't be trusted'. Even without realizing it, they keep emotional walls up, test the people who care about them and often choose partners who confirm their old belief.

Or someone may want strong health and high energy, but hold the belief, 'My genes are bad' or 'I never stick to routines'. So, they begin enthusiastically, but the moment they miss one workout or one healthy meal, their old identity takes over and they quietly quit.

The pattern is simple: **when your beliefs are misaligned with your goals, your actions become hesitant and your results stay inconsistent.** Your life cannot outrun your deepest beliefs.

Examine, Update, Upgrade

History gives us a powerful reminder of this. Centuries ago, most of the world believed the Earth was flat. When Galileo suggested that the Earth was spherical—and later, that it revolved around the Sun—he was mocked, resisted and even imprisoned. His truth challenged the world's most deeply held beliefs. And yet, he was right.

The lesson? **Just because a belief is widely accepted doesn't mean it's correct.** Sometimes, what the *whole world* believes can still be wrong and what *you* quietly believe can be right. The same is true inside you.

Many of your current beliefs are not facts. They are just old mental hand-me-downs from your childhood, your culture, your surroundings or the environment you grew up in. They can be about anything: your abilities, your worth, your relationships, religions, political parties, countries, etc.

But here's the key: **beliefs are not meant to be inherited forever. They are meant to be examined, updated and upgraded.**

If a belief is helping you grow, keep it. If it's holding you back, it's time to question it. Because staying loyal to old beliefs can cost you new possibilities.

What Happens When Your Belief Changes

Sometimes, all it takes is **one moment** for a belief to shift, and when your belief changes, your life changes with it.

Take the example of **Raja Nayak**, a Bengaluru-based entrepreneur and social worker. There was a time when he sold shirts on the footpath to survive. Born into poverty and facing layers of social stigma as a Dalit, he grew up surrounded by limiting messages about what he could and could not become.

Then one evening, while watching Amitabh Bachchan's movie *Trishul*, something cracked open inside him. The hero's resilience and determination stirred something deeper, a new belief: *'If he can rise, so can I.'*

That single spark reshaped his life. Today, Raja Nayak has a net worth of over Rs 60 crore, owns several businesses and runs educational institutions for underprivileged children. **One movie didn't just entertain him; it rewrote his inner script.**

Beliefs can shift in countless ways—through a movie, a song, a book, a podcast, a powerful story, a meaningful conversation, meeting someone inspiring or even visiting a place that opens your perspective.

When **Ritesh Agarwal**, the founder of OYO, came to my podcast, I asked him about a defining moment in his journey. He spoke about the time he was selected for the prestigious **Thiel Fellowship**, started by entrepreneur–

investor Peter Thiel. There, he found himself surrounded by people who were building bold ideas at a very young age. That environment, those conversations and Peter Thiel's mentorship completely reshaped how he looked at business, risk and ambition. He said it opened his mind to a world far bigger than he had imagined before. **It didn't just give him tools; it gave him a new belief about what was possible for him.**

Sometimes, it's not even a single person—it's an entire **environment** that shifts your belief system.

During my podcast conversation with **Azhar Iqbal**, the co-founder of Inshorts, I asked him what first sparked his desire to become an entrepreneur. He told me that he grew up in a small village, where entrepreneurship wasn't even a visible concept. But when he entered IIT Delhi, he suddenly found himself surrounded by innovation, ambition and possibility. He discovered that **Sachin Bansal and Binny Bansal—the founders of Flipkart—were alumni of the same institute.** That realization changed everything. *'If they could build something massive starting here,'* he thought, *'why can't I?'* That shift in belief became the foundation for building Inshorts.

Reprogramming Your Beliefs

Beliefs may feel fixed, but they are not. They are **fluid, rewritable and upgradeable.** And when your belief changes, your thoughts change, your actions change and your future changes.

Before we begin, I want to say this clearly: **reprogramming your beliefs does not mean you are broken, weak or failing.**

In fact, the very reason you are reading a book about transforming your life shows that you already hold some incredible beliefs, like believing in growth, in change and in your ability to create a better future.

Those empowering beliefs have brought you this far. But growth, as we've discussed before, is not a switch you flip once. It is a journey. And on this journey, we must keep updating our beliefs, just like updating an old map when you discover better roads.

Identifying Your Limiting Beliefs

If you're not fully sure what your limiting beliefs are, don't worry. Most people aren't. Here's a quick way to uncover them.

Mirror Moment: Be honest with yourself as you answer these three questions:

1. **What are the negative thoughts I often say about myself?**

    Dig deep. It could be things like: *'I don't look good . . . I'm not confident . . . I can't speak on stage . . . I'm not smart enough . . . I'm not creative . . . I don't have strong willpower . . . I'm too shy . . .'*

    _____
    _____
    _____
    _____
    _____

2. **What excuses usually stop me from taking action?**

    For example: *'I don't have enough time . . . It's not the right time . . . I don't know the right people . . . People like me can't succeed in this . . .'*

    _____
    _____
    _____
    _____
    _____

3. ***What fears or doubts come up when I imagine achieving my goals?***
   Maybe it's: *'People will judge me . . . I'll lose my peace of mind . . . I won't be able to balance everything . . . I'll have to sacrifice happiness to be successful . . .'*

   _____
   _____
   _____
   _____

When you answer these questions honestly, you'll see a list of sentences or patterns emerging. **This is your list of limiting beliefs.**

Don't get overwhelmed if you spot many. Remember, you also have powerful beliefs within you and you don't need to change all limiting beliefs at once. Just pick **one core belief** that you feel is holding you back the most. One belief that, if you change it, could unlock massive growth in your life.

That's where we'll start. We'll work on **that one belief together**, understand how to rewrite it and once you learn the method, you'll be able to use it again and again to transform any area of your life.

Replacing Your Limiting Beliefs: The 3E Method

By now, you've identified one core limiting belief that quietly holds you back. To understand this process better, let's take a common example:

'I'm not smart enough to be wealthy.'

Your belief might be completely different, but as you read, simply apply the same steps to your own belief.

If you've carried a belief like this for years, it may feel permanent, but here's the truth: **beliefs are not facts. They are patterns. And patterns can be rewritten.**

Over the years, I've read countless books on belief, spoken to some of the world's leading life coaches and worked closely with hundreds of people in one-to-one coaching. So, I distilled everything I learned into a simple, practical framework—the **3E Formula**. It is a method anyone can use to transform their limiting beliefs into empowering ones.

E1: Emotion

Our brain doesn't know the difference between imagination and reality. For example, if I keep talking about your favourite food, say **rajma–chawal,** and mention it repeatedly, describing its aroma and taste, you'll soon find yourself salivating even though it's not actually there.

The same thing happens with beliefs. If your mind has imagined that *'I'm not worthy of wealth'*, it starts feeling real because your emotions have accepted it as truth.

So why not use this same power to build a better truth?

- Visualize the **wealthy version of you**: confidently building, creating, contributing.
- Feel the emotions that come with it: pride, security, freedom, excitement.
- Speak it out: 'Wealth is a skill and I can learn any skill I commit to.'

Emotion rewires belief faster than logic. Because once your body starts **feeling** the new belief, your mind starts **believing** it.

(We'll explore this in much greater depth when we talk about **neuro-manifestation** in the next chapter, where you'll learn how to completely reprogram your subconscious mind)

E2: *Experience*

Many of your old beliefs were formed through past experiences—childhood incidents, early failures or stories from people around you. But you can create **new experiences** to instil new beliefs.

When I began public speaking, I didn't start on big stages. I gave myself the experience of speaking to small groups first. Each small win rewired my belief that *'I can do this'*.

Similarly, if you think *'I'm not smart enough to be wealthy'*,

- Start small projects to see results on a small scale.
- Take a financial education workshop.
- Track small wins daily to build confidence.

Every time you prove your brain wrong with experience, your belief starts shifting.

E3: Environment

Your environment is like the soil where your beliefs grow. If the soil is poor, the best seeds won't survive. But today, you have the power to change your mental environment instantly.

- Read biographies of people who became rich through learning, not inheritance.
- Listen to podcasts, join communities and follow people who normalise growth, learning, and wealth-building.

- Surround yourself—even virtually—with people whose presence makes your dreams feel possible.

We are fortunate to live in an era where a single phone can connect you to any environment you want. Use it wisely. If your surroundings don't support your dreams, **build new surroundings digitally.**

When you work on your **Emotion, Experience** and **Environment** consistently, you can transform any limiting belief into an empowering one. And once your beliefs change, your actions change, and so does your life.

E for Empowerment comes from the 3 Es: Emotion, Experience, Environment.

Mirror Moment: Write one Limiting belief along with your 3E Plan to replace it with an empowering belief.

Limiting Belief: _____

New Belief: _____

Emotion: _____

Experience: _____

Environment: _____

Conclusion

Looking back, every breakthrough I've had—from rebuilding my life after financial collapse, to starting my YouTube channel against every odd, to impacting millions—came down to one thing: **belief**. Not blind optimism, but a conscious decision to back myself when no one else would. Your belief is the invisible force that keeps the engine alive when everything else stalls.

You've now seen how beliefs are formed, how they shape your actions and how they can be rewritten. And when that shift happens, even slightly, it changes everything. Because belief is not just an idea in your mind; it's the foundation of your reality.

If you ever find yourself doubting, remember this: **you don't need anyone else's permission.** The moment you decide to believe differently, you begin to live differently.

In the next chapters, we'll go even deeper—learning how to rewire your subconscious, align your thoughts with your vision and turn your new beliefs into tangible results. Because belief is the seed, but action, alignment and consistency are what make it bloom.

So, as you close this chapter, give yourself that permission slip.

Believe, not because the world says so, but because your future deserves it.

Chapter 7

Manifestation Decoded

Think about the last time you set a goal with full enthusiasm. Maybe it was to get fit, start a business or learn a new skill. In the beginning, you were excited, supercharged with motivation. But as days passed, distractions crept in, old habits resurfaced, and suddenly, that fire didn't burn as bright.

This happens to most people because motivation is temporary. That's why successful people use reinforcement techniques to stay on track.

When I set a few ambitious goals on 1 January 2019—writing a book, creating a YouTube channel, earning the silver button, then the gold button—things started to happen. I had a fair idea about how laws of attraction and manifestation work.

I knew that excitement alone wouldn't be enough. I needed something to keep my vision alive every single day. That's when I discovered the power of reinforcement. So, I found pictures related to my goals and created my vision board. When I actually started to be successful, I realized how powerful it was!

My goals were 100 times beyond my net worth then. Yet, I was able to achieve it all.

Why am I sharing this with you? It is not to convince you of the power of manifestation, visualization or the subconscious mind, but to offer my journey as 'proof'. Call it the laws of attraction, subconscious programming or manifestation, but know that there is a science behind it all.

When you set ambitious goals, your mind plays a crucial role in making them a reality.

Manifestation Is Not Magic

Let's clear a common myth right away: **manifestation is not about wishful thinking.** It's not about closing your eyes, visualizing your dream and waiting for magic to happen. It's not about creating a vision board once and forgetting it. And it's definitely not about forcing the universe to hand over what you want.

Real manifestation is not magic; **it's neuroscience.** It's about how your mind filters, processes and responds to information. It's about how your brain starts aligning your thoughts, emotions and actions toward what you repeatedly focus on.

To understand this, let's talk about one of the most fascinating systems in your brain: the **reticular activating system (RAS).** It acts as your mind's filter, deciding what deserves your attention and what doesn't.

Let me explain with a few examples.

Imagine you're planning a trip to Goa with your friends. A few days later, you are invited to a party where different groups are engaged in conversations, laughter and chatter. The room is filled with voices, creating a background hum.

But then, amidst the crowd, you overhear two people discussing a topic: a trip to Goa. It's something you've already been thinking about, and suddenly, their conversation stands out while the rest fades into the background. What just happened?

Until that moment, everything was indistinct noise. But the moment your mind recognized something personally relevant, you tuned in. This is a perfect example of how our brain filters information, dismissing the irrelevant while amplifying what aligns with our thoughts and interests.

That's your **RAS** at work: it filters thousands of sounds around you and highlights only what your brain finds *important* at that moment.

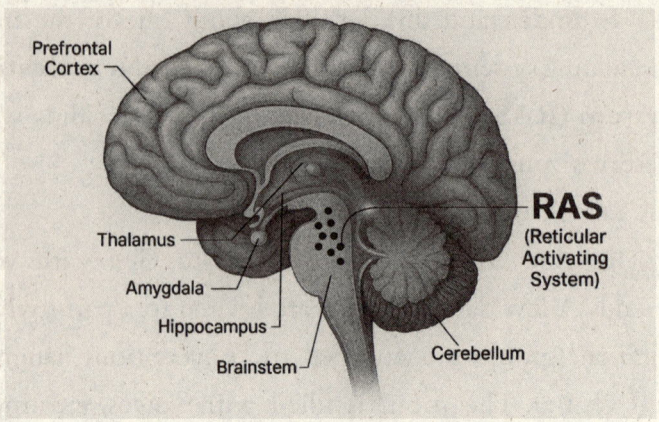

Here's another example. Suppose you've decided to buy a **red car** of a particular model. Suddenly, you start noticing that car everywhere. You see its ad on a billboard, spot the same colour at traffic lights and notice it in the parking lot. The truth is that those cars were always there. You just weren't *noticing* them before.

And this doesn't just apply to cars or trips. Let's say your name is **Sahil** and you're driving down a busy road full of shops and hoardings. Amidst all that visual noise, your eyes instantly pick out a board that says, 'Hotel Sahil' or 'Sahil Traders'. Why? Because your RAS recognizes it as *personally relevant*.

Every second, your brain receives millions of bits of information—sounds, visuals, words, sensations. But your conscious mind can process only a small fraction of it.

How the RAS Works

The **reticular activating system (RAS)** is a network of neurons located at the base of your brain, acting as a powerful gatekeeper between your conscious and subconscious mind. Every second, millions of pieces of information enter your senses: what you see, hear, touch and feel. But your conscious brain can only handle a small portion of that data.

So, the RAS decides what deserves your attention. And what determines its decision? **Your dominant thoughts, emotions and beliefs.**

Think of your RAS as the search engine of your brain. Whatever keyword you feed it—through thoughts, emotions and repetition—it begins to 'search' for matching experiences and opportunities in your real world.

For instance, if you think that you are under-confident, you will have selective reception of what can help you become under-confident.

Whereas, if you believe that you are meant to drive a Merc, or to become a millionaire, or to fund 100 students, your mind will keep working on 'how to achieve that goal'.

If you don't feed your mind, it will go on auto-pilot mode, but if you do, it will go on controlled mode. That's the difference.

Here's the powerful part: your RAS doesn't just passively filter reality; it actively reinforces your focus. The more you visualize something with emotion and clarity, the more your RAS begins to align your attention, decisions and even your body language toward making it real.

This is the true science behind manifestation. It's not about forcing the universe to bend to your will; it's about training your brain to notice and act upon the opportunities that have always been around you. Manifestation begins not in the stars, but in your **neural filters**—the patterns of thought you choose to strengthen every day.

How Does RAS Help?

1. More Focus and Concentration

Your mind doesn't get distracted by irrelevant details. Instead, it sharpens its focus and aligns your thoughts towards your goal.

Our subconscious is incredibly powerful. Let me share a personal example. I programmed my mind to become an impactful life coach. This single thought shaped my perception of the world around me. Books that I read seemed to highlight sections that could help me in my coaching and trainings. Even while watching stand-up comedy, I found myself analysing the artist's stage presence, timing and delivery rather than just laughing at the jokes. My brain had automatically started filtering information that aligned with my goal.

That's how the focus of our mind changes. It shifts towards things that bring us closer to what we truly desire.

2. Sustainable Motivation

Motivation tends to fade over time, but when you have strong mental anchors, it stays with you.

Take **Bruce Lee**, for instance. He once wrote a letter to himself stating that within ten years, he would become the most successful and 'highest-paid Oriental superstar' in the US. That letter, which is on display in a museum today, was his personal manifesto. Despite facing physical challenges, he achieved exactly what he had envisioned, that too within the timeline he had set for himself.

You can also consider the case of **Jim Carrey**. The son of a janitor who barely made ends meet, he wrote himself a $10 million cheque dated to ten years later. At that time, it seemed absurd. His family lived in a van, and everyone around him doubted his dreams and did everything to discourage him. But Jim kept that cheque in his wallet and kept looking at it for 'inspiration'.

That constant reminder reinforced his belief in himself. And as we all know today, not only did he achieve that goal, but he far surpassed it.

This is **the magic of visual reminders**. They help keep you motivated, even when circumstances seem unfavourable.

3. Strengthens Confidence

Visualization is a tool that strengthens confidence before you even step into the real situation.

In 2012, Virat Kohli faced a rough patch in his career. After two underwhelming matches in Australia, he had a conversation with himself and decided to adopt a new approach: **visualization**. He started imagining each ball coming towards him and strategized his shots, seeing himself perform flawlessly.

The results were immediately apparent in his very next match.

His performance improved significantly, and since then, visualization has become a core part of his mental training. He often talks about the power of the mind and how picturing success before it happens builds an unshakable belief in oneself.

The same principle applies to anyone stepping onto a stage for the first time. If you have mentally rehearsed your performance countless times, by the time you actually do it, it feels familiar and effortless. That's why great speakers, athletes and performers seem so confident—they've already played the scenario in their minds a hundred times before facing the audience.

4. Boosts Creativity and Ideation

Did you know how Nikola Tesla, one of the greatest inventors of all time, got his ideas?

He relied on the power of his subconscious mind. He would hold an idea in his head and let his mind work on it, refining and perfecting it until it was ready for execution. Some of his most groundbreaking innovations, such as turbines and wireless electricity, were born in the depths of his mind before ever being put to paper.

Tesla even stated that most of his thinking happened during sleep, proving how powerful the subconscious truly is.

5. Amplifies Problem-Solving

Your subconscious mind isn't just a storage unit, it's an active problem-solving engine that works silently in the background, shaping your ideas and bringing them to life.

Sometime ago, I met **Aakash Anand, founder of BellaVita**, at an event. We instantly connected and became good friends. We even did a podcast together. During our conversation, he revealed something fascinating about his belief in visualization.

He once wrote 'Rs 25 crore' on a piece of paper and stuck it on his bedroom wall, along with images of his dream house, the car and the lifestyle he wanted to achieve with that money. Every single day, he looked at those visuals.

At the time, achieving that figure seemed impossible. But as months passed, opportunities started aligning. His company grew exponentially, and soon, he wasn't just looking at the number, he was living it.

This is how visualization works.

It aligns your thoughts with the actions needed to make your dreams real. When your brain is repeatedly exposed to an idea, it starts finding ways to make it happen, often in ways you never imagined before.

That is when there is no space for laziness or procrastination. Your mind keeps changing your ways of working when it is focused. Instead of solely listening to music during an hour's drive, you would switch to forty-five minutes of a podcast and give the rest to music. Gradually, you will keep reaching a step closer to your goal.

6. Supports Habit Formation

Imagine a young man sitting in a small village in Austria, thousands of miles away from the US. In his dimly lit room, he stares at posters of bodybuilders and Hollywood stars, visualizing himself among them. Day after day, those images fuel his ambition.

That young man was **Arnold Schwarzenegger**.

Through sheer visualization and relentless pursuit, he turned his dreams into reality, becoming Mr Universe (7 times), Mr Olympia (5 times) and the top Hollywood star of his time.

But he didn't stop there.

He went on to become the governor of California, twice. The only thing that kept him from becoming the President of the United States was the constitutional rule barring non-American-born citizens from holding the office.

What made this incredible journey possible? Those posters.

They weren't just decorations on his wall, they were daily reminders of his goals, potential and future self. They conditioned his mind, reinforced his focus and built the habits that shaped his legendary career.

We Need Reminders

Everyone knows Coca Cola. Still wherever you see, you will find an advertisement running, whether on television, a hoarding or even the banners in a stadium.

Or think of Colgate for that matter. Everyone knows Colgate, and is aware of its function. The company still keeps running ads.

These brands keep spending billions of dollars every year on the advertisement of their products. Why do they do that?

The answer is 'reminders'.

These companies understand that the product that remains in front of the customer's eyes will be in their minds. Next time, when they go to buy a soft drink, the first name that comes to their mind will be Coca Cola—or Colgate, if they need toothpaste. These know that their reminders will keep on influencing people's actions. That is the reason why they have been spending a fortune to keep you reminded of their names.

As others are gaining profit due to their RAS, is it not high time that you also start gaining from your own RAS?

And to achieve that, we need reminders. This is where two important tools, visualization and affirmations come into play.

It's not that only those who practised affirmations found success, nor is it true that those who didn't failed.

It's not that only those who visualized their goals achieved them, nor that those who didn't were unsuccessful.

Some people are naturally confident, while others develop confidence through deliberate practice.

Some people unconsciously attract opportunities into their lives, while others consciously train their minds to do so.

But here's the difference—reminders act as a catalyst. They give you momentum, focus and a 10x multiplier.

What might take five years to achieve can be accomplished in much lesser time if visualization and affirmations become part of your daily routine. This isn't just theory. It is a personal experience. And I'm not alone in this belief. Because I actively study, listen and observe, I have seen countless successful individuals confirm the same.

Don't just take my word for it. Test it!

Activating Your RAS

Once you understand how your reticular activating system works, the next step is to train it consciously. Think of your

RAS as your personal assistant—ready to filter the world for what truly matters to you. But like any assistant, it performs only when you give it *clear instructions, emotional conviction* and *consistent reminders*.

You must **feed** your RAS with clarity by telling it *exactly* what you want, not vague statements like 'I want to be rich' or 'I just want to be happy'. Give it detail—paint a vivid picture of your ideal life, income or health.

Then, **fuel** it with emotion. Your RAS listens not to logic but to feeling. When you connect your goals with enthusiasm, gratitude and excitement, your brain tags them as important and begins to notice every signal related to them.

Finally, **reinforce** it through repetition. The more you revisit your vision, affirm it and talk about it, the stronger your neural circuits become. Every repetition is like pressing 'save' in your mind's software—gradually turning intention into instinct.

Once these three are in place, visualization and affirmations start working like magic—not because of superstition, but because your mind is neurologically wired to notice, act and align.

The Power of Visualization

Visualization isn't about fantasy—it's mental rehearsal. When you visualize your goals vividly and repeatedly, your brain begins to build neural connections as if you've *already lived* that reality. That's why athletes rehearse their moves mentally, and why leaders and artists visualize success before they experience it.

I've practised this for years and it has completely transformed my performance. When I began visualizing my goals daily, something shifted inside me. Excuses quietly turned into responsibility. My conversations started reflecting my vision. I began attracting ideas, people and opportunities aligned with my goals. Every morning when I visualized, it felt like a mental warm-up session. By the time I reached the office or the studio, I was already switched on: energized, solution-oriented and clear.

That's how I've been able to consistently create over **1000+ long-form videos**, **thousands of reels**, **multiple businesses** and **a strong, motivated team** without losing inspiration. Visualization became my *mental fuel*.

And the best part? There isn't just one way to visualize. You can:

- Close your eyes and imagine your dream life vividly.
- Create a **vision board** in your room filled with pictures of your goals.
- Make a **WhatsApp group** with only yourself, where you post photos representing your future.
- Record a **voice note** describing your ideal life and listen to it daily.

Choose whatever works best for you—whether you're a visual, auditory or reading-based learner. What matters most is consistency. Because every time you visualize your desired future, you remind your mind what to work towards—and your RAS starts aligning everything around you to make it real.

The Power of Affirmations

When I first heard coaches and trainers talk about affirmations, I didn't quite understand the function and usefulness of saying things to myself each morning.

But as I grew as a coach, my mentors, trainers and even books repeatedly emphasized the same thing. So, I decided to test it. And when I did, I finally understood the science behind it.

For example, when I attend networking events and sit with CEOs and founders, they often ask me, 'How do you manage to get things done without ever raising your voice?'

The answer lies in one of my fifteen daily affirmations: 'I lead my team with love.'

Since I remind myself of this every day, my subconscious mind constantly finds ways to get things done without resorting to anger or frustration. I have an expectation, yes, but I refuse to let it disturb my happiness. With a growth mindset, I explore different approaches to handling situations while staying true to my values.

I wasn't always a good listener, but I affirmed myself daily to improve at it.

There was a time when we suffered huge financial loss. There were other tough moments, too. But every single day, I repeated these words to myself:

I am a powerful and impactful coach.

And that is what kept me moving forward.

Why Should You Try It?

Attending training programmes or reading books is not enough. You will end up asking yourself, 'what next?'. Because this much is not going to help you achieve your goals.

If you don't give a reminder to yourself daily, you will eventually forget about everything you were so determined to do.

Having a training session will help you 'knock' your twenty-five-year-old beliefs, but they will change only when there are regular reminders.

Affirmations help us stay tuned, stay focused and maintain a controlled thought process. Because at the end of the day, reminders influence our actions.

If you're wondering whether affirmations work, test it for yourself!

After all, you will agree that affirmations are not going to harm you in any way. If something doesn't harm us but has the potential to benefit us, why not give it a try? I tested it, so I suggest you do the same. Let me make the process easy for you so that you don't make mistakes during your testing.

6 Ps of Affirmation

Let me introduce you to the **6 Ps of Affirmations**, a simple yet powerful way to make them truly effective.

1. Possible:

If you don't believe in your affirmations, they won't work. If something seems impossible to you, even repeating it won't bring results. So, ensure your affirmations feel achievable and within reach.

2. Power

Your affirmations should reflect your own power, not someone else's. For example:

Wrong: *'My team is working passionately.'* (Power is with others.)

Right: *'I am igniting passion and commitment in my team.'* (Power stays with me.)

3. Present

Always phrase affirmations in the present tense, not the future. Your subconscious mind works best when it hears things in the now, reinforcing immediate action. For example:

'I eat nutritious food' as opposed to *'I will eat nutritious food'*.

4. Personal

Every affirmation should begin with 'I' because transformation starts from within. Affirmations like *'I am strong'*, *'I am confident'*, or *'I am growing every day'* reinforce your personal commitment.

5. Positive

Your mind doesn't differentiate between reality and thought; it only responds to the *emotion* behind your words. Remember what we discussed in the previous chapter: every word you speak carries a feeling.

So when you say, *'I am not afraid of public speaking,'* your mind still focuses on the word *afraid* and activates the emotion of fear. But when you reframe it to *'I am becoming a confident speaker,'* you're sending your mind a completely different message, one filled with courage and assurance. Always choose words that carry the feeling you want to experience, not the one you're trying to avoid.

6. Passion: Your affirmations should align with what excites and drives you. When you're passionate about something, your affirmations become more powerful and impactful.

By following these 6 Ps, you ensure your affirmations aren't just words, but a powerful tool to shape your mindset and actions.

Mirror Moment: Write Affirmations for yourself using 6Ps:
_____
_____
_____
_____
_____

Conclusion

Manifestation isn't about forcing outcomes; it's about aligning your inner world so strongly that your outer world has no choice but to follow.

Your brain is already working day and night—filtering, sorting and shaping your experiences. The only question is: what instructions are you giving it?

When you feed your mind clarity, emotion and repetition, your reticular activating system starts working for you, not against you. You stop chasing luck and start creating alignment.

Every time you visualize, you are rehearsing your future. Every time you affirm, you are programming your belief. And every time you stay consistent, you are re-wiring your destiny.

So, don't wait for miracles. **Train your mind to become the miracle.**

In the next chapter, we'll decode how to translate these inner signals into real-world action: the bridge between your dreams and your results.

Chapter 8

The Magic of Momentum

The 100 Letters

Back in 2012, long before my paid speaking career began, I decided to take my first real step toward my dream. I wrote letters—yes, actual letters—to more than a hundred colleges, offering to conduct a *free motivational session* for their students. My goal was simple: to inspire young minds, help them deal with stress and prepare them for their careers.

Weeks passed with little response until one university near Jaipur invited me. Excited, I travelled there with great enthusiasm, imagining a hall full of students eager to learn. But when I reached, I realized a college fest was going on—there were food stalls, music and a DJ playing nearby. After three or four reminders to the organizers, they finally arranged something for me. Five students were asked to sit on chairs while loud music played in the background. That was my 'seminar'.

It wasn't the beginning I had imagined, but I spoke anyway—with all my heart.

Later, another college in Meerut called me for a 'guest lecture'. I soon realized they weren't really interested in student learning; they just wanted to tick a box in their curriculum report. Still, I delivered my best. Then came Lovely Professional University in Jalandhar, where I was welcomed into a packed auditorium. The energy was electric. I also spoke at RBMI Bareilly, another memorable experience with an audience of two hundred students.

Out of the hundred letters I had sent, only four colleges responded. Two were disappointing. Two were life-changing. But every single one moved me forward.

Those early sessions gave me confidence, photographs and credibility. They became my first step toward building a professional speaking career. I went from speaking for free to charging Rs 5000 . . . then Rs 10,000 . . . then Rs 50,000 . . . and today, my sessions are valued in lakhs.

All of this started with *one simple action*: sending those letters.

I often remind my audiences: **any action is better than inaction.** Inaction keeps you stuck where you are; action, no matter how small, creates momentum.

I'm reminded of what Azhar Iqbal, the co-founder of Inshorts, once shared with me. Today, Inshorts is one of India's most popular news apps, delivering short, crisp updates that millions read every day. But when Azhar published his very first news shot, it was filled with grammatical errors. His English wasn't perfect, but he didn't wait for perfection. He started anyway. Ironically, the same app that began with broken English now helps thousands improve theirs!

That's the power of starting.

Think about it.

- You can dream of becoming a writer, but until you pick up the pen, it remains just a dream.
- You can envision a fit, healthy body, but unless you start moving, nothing changes.
- You can set the goal to grow in your career, but unless you take steps—learning, networking or upskilling—it remains just a wish.

Every great journey begins with an imperfect step. Every breakthrough begins with a moment of courage. Because when you move, life moves with you. Any action is better than inaction.

Mirror Moment: Think of one action you've been postponing because you're waiting for the 'perfect time' or 'perfect plan'. Write it down and take the first small step toward it today.

_____

_____

The Thrill of Being Uncomfortable

We all know that *action* is important. We all know what to do. By now, in this journey, **you already know what you want in your life** and you even have an idea of the steps that will take you there.

Yet, the biggest difference between people who succeed and people who stay stuck isn't knowledge, it's *action*.

In my workshops and training programmes, I often ask participants,

'What stops you from taking action?'

Or

'Why do you start something with energy but struggle to continue?'

The answers are usually the same: *I lose motivation . . . I procrastinate . . . I'm lazy . . . I'm scared . . . I get stuck in my comfort zone.*

Let me share a story with you from my childhood that you might relate to.

When I was in Class 9, I had a crush on a girl named Simran. One summer evening, I saw her cycling past my house with her friends. For the first time, she wasn't in her school uniform, she was wearing a blue top and jeans. To my fourteen-year-old self, that moment felt magical.

Later, I discovered that she attended a tuition class nearby. So, every afternoon, I made it a ritual to stand outside my house around 3.30 p.m., pretending to be busy, just to catch a glimpse of her cycling by. She'd smile, I'd smile back, and that was enough to keep me floating the rest of the day.

She'd return around 5.30, and I'd be there again, standing in the heat, waiting for another brief smile. I did this for weeks.

Now think about it. It was scorching hot. I was sweating. I was uncomfortable. But did I care? Not at all. Because I was emotionally *charged*.

That's how human behaviour works. When we love something, we don't call it *discomfort*, we call it *excitement*.

When a relationship is new, we talk on the phone for hours without sleep. When a new game hooks us, we sit for hours in the same chair without a complaint. When a trip is coming up, we stay awake all night packing with enthusiasm. We willingly do things that are *uncomfortable* and even enjoy them, because we are emotionally connected.

Now imagine applying that same energy to your goals.

What if you could fall in love with your discomfort? What if learning a new skill felt as thrilling as waiting for that one smile? What if staying consistent on your dream felt as exciting as planning a trip?

The truth is, **you're not lazy, you're just not emotionally connected yet.** Discomfort isn't your enemy; indifference is.

The moment you attach emotion to your action, discomfort becomes drive. And that's when procrastination disappears, laziness fades and progress becomes natural. Because in the end, it's not about avoiding discomfort; it's about *enjoying* it.

Is it All Worth it?

Why push ourselves? Why not stay where we are—safe, comfortable, untouched by struggle? Why take all the pain, all the effort, all the action?

To answer that, imagine two tiny seeds lying side by side in the soil.

The first seed says, 'It's cozy here. I'm safe, warm and protected. Why should I change? Why go through darkness, pressure and storms? I'll stay right here.'

The second seed whispers, 'I was born for more. I don't know how tall I'll grow, but I'm willing to find out.'

And so, the second seed begins its journey. It breaks open—yes, painfully—pushing through the heavy soil. It faces darkness, crushing weight, scorching sunlight, fierce winds and endless rain. But it keeps growing. Slowly, courageously, beautifully.

Over time, that seed becomes a magnificent tree. It provides shade to travellers, nests to birds, fruits to people. It bends in storms but stands tall again. It witnesses sunsets, rainbows and seasonal change. It lives a *big* life—full of struggle, yes, but also full of meaning.

The first seed, meanwhile, stays underground: safe, comfortable and untouched. But as years pass, it begins to rot. And before it fades away, it whispers, 'I could have been that tree. I was born for that too.'

Both seeds experienced pain: one the **pain of growth**, the other the **pain of regret**. But only one lived.

That's our story too. Each of us has immense potential within. We can choose to stay buried under our fears, doubts and excuses, or we can break open, grow through discomfort and become the fullest version of ourselves.

The pain of growth is temporary. The pain of regret lasts a lifetime.

So, if you must choose pain, choose the one that helps you rise. Choose the one that gives you stories, experiences and memories to cherish. Choose the one that makes you look back one day and say, *'Yes, it was all worth it.'*

Immunity to Discomfort: The Stoic Secret

The ability to take action consistently doesn't just come from motivation, it comes from mental flexibility. And one of the best philosophies that taught this centuries ago is Stoicism, a school of thought practiced by kings, philosophers and warriors alike.

Stoicism teaches that pain, uncertainty and discomfort are not enemies, they are training partners. The Stoics believed that if you want to build strength of mind, you must practise facing discomfort in small, intentional doses.

Even the wealthiest Roman emperors like Marcus Aurelius or Seneca—who had every luxury available—would intentionally sleep on hard floors, wear simple clothes or eat plain food for a few days. Why? Because they knew comfort makes the mind fragile. When life throws unexpected storms, only the flexible mind survives.

They believed that by exposing yourself to temporary discomfort, you train your brain to stop panicking when things don't go your way. It's like building an emotional muscle—the more you stretch it, the more resilient it becomes.

When your mind learns that discomfort doesn't kill you—it simply stretches you—it starts becoming fearless. And a fearless mind finds it easier to act.

Now, you don't have to meditate in the mountains or walk barefoot on ice to build this resilience. You can start small, with simple, everyday challenges that gently push you out of your comfort zone.

Here are a few ways to begin building your 'immunity to discomfort':

- Skip instant comfort. Fast for a day or give up sugar or junk food for a week.
- Limit digital noise. Try staying off Instagram for forty-eight hours or set a daily screen limit.
- Create a self-control challenge. Fix a spending cap for the month or resist buying something you don't really need.

These small acts may look ordinary, but each one tells your brain: 'I am in control'. And that message rewires your inner world faster than any motivational quote ever can.

When your brain regularly experiences small discomforts, it stops resisting big ones. You become calmer under pressure. You stop overthinking and start doing.

Because here's the truth: **action becomes easy for a flexible mind**. When you stop fearing discomfort, you stop postponing life.

Mirror Moment: What would your life look like five years from now if you started embracing discomfort today?

_____

_____

Conclusion

You've now seen how action beats hesitation, how discomfort shapes strength and how resilience builds mastery. The truth is, no one is born fearless or endlessly motivated. We build courage by moving—one small, imperfect step at a time.

Every time you choose action over overthinking, you train your mind to trust you a little more. Every time you stretch beyond comfort, you remind yourself that you can grow through anything. And every time you show up despite fear, you create proof, not for the world, but for yourself.

Momentum is magic. Once you start rolling, the universe starts moving with you. Doors open. People appear. Clarity unfolds. Not because fate changes, but because *you* do.

In the end, it's not talent, luck or timing that separates dreamers from doers. It's the courage to begin, the strength to continue and the wisdom to know that **every small action counts.**

Start today. And let motion become your momentum.

Chapter 9

Daily Mastery: 21 Days

Have you ever noticed how fired up we feel after reading a great book, attending a powerful workshop or watching an inspiring video? In that moment, everything feels possible. We're full of ideas, ready to act, ready to change.

But then, a few days later, the spark fades. The fire that once burned bright turns into a flicker. Motivation dips. Energy drops. Life takes over.

In my early years as a trainer, this pattern bothered me deeply. Corporate clients would often tell me, *'Our team performed exceptionally well after your session, but after a week or two, things went back to normal.'* Individuals who attended my programmes said the same—that initial burst of motivation was strong, but it didn't last long.

I kept asking myself, 'Why does this happen? Why does the fire fade?'

I experimented for years, tested multiple approaches and finally discovered what truly creates lasting transformation. The answer was simple but profound: **Daily Mastery.**

The Power of Every Day

I've always drawn inspiration from sports, especially from athletes who understand the value of consistent performance.

Imagine a cricket match. One ball left. Four runs needed. The batsman hits a boundary, and the team wins. The crowd cheers, commentators go wild and we call it a 'match-winning shot'.

But let's think deeper. Did that *one ball* really win the match? No. That ball decided the result, but every ball before it *contributed* to that moment. Every run, every catch, every over, every single delivery—each one mattered.

That's how life works too.

The day you achieve your dream—get your dream job, meet your life partner, buy your first house, or land your biggest client—feels like a 'winning day'. But that day didn't just happen. It was built by hundreds of unseen days, the days when you woke up early, pushed through doubt, stayed disciplined, kept learning and refused to quit.

Your life is shaped not by the extraordinary days, but by the ordinary ones you master. Each day is like a ball in your personal match; it may not make headlines, but it decides your destiny.

That's the power of Daily Mastery. When you master your day, you master your direction. When you win each small moment, the big victories take care of themselves.

Daily Review

Have you ever wondered why large organizations grow into billion-dollar empires while most individuals struggle to stay consistent with their own goals? The answer lies in one word: **organization.**

The word *organization* itself comes from being *organized*—through systems, processes and regular reviews. That's what allows one person at the top to lead hundreds, and hundreds to manage thousands, all moving in the same direction with clarity and purpose.

When a company runs like a well-oiled machine, it's not luck; it's structure. Every task, every target, every team member is connected through a chain of accountability and review.

Now imagine this: If an employee isn't reviewed regularly by their team leader, and the team leader isn't reviewed by the manager. If the department heads aren't reviewed by the CEO, and the CEO isn't reviewed by the board. What will happen? The organization will start drifting. There will be confusion, low morale, missed goals, and eventually, collapse.

Reviews are what keep an organization alive. They ensure that actions are being tracked, feedback is being shared, corrections are being made and growth is being celebrated.

Now, here's the insight that changed my life: **if consistent reviews can turn thousands of people into a high-performing organization, what could regular self-review do for *you*?**

What if *you* became your own organization? What if you built your own systems, processes, and most importantly, your own *review mechanism*?

You've already come far. You've understood your belief system, manifestation process and action steps. Now comes the most critical element that ties everything together: **self-review.**

Your check-in with yourself is your personal board meeting. It's where you measure, reflect and reset. It's the moment where you ask, *'Am I still moving in the right direction?'*

This daily review makes you your own coach—one who doesn't just motivate you once in a while, but keeps you accountable *every single day*. And when you have a coach working with you every day, your growth becomes inevitable.

That's exactly what I'm going to help you build next—your personal **Morning and Evening Review Practice.** It is a simple yet powerful routine that has changed thousands of lives, including mine.

I call this your **Daily Mastery Practice**, and if you've come this far in the book, I want you to give this next exercise a fair chance.

For the next twenty-one days, follow this system exactly as I'll describe. No shortcuts, no tweaks—just twenty-one days of pure commitment.

Trust me, at the end of these three weeks, you'll meet a version of yourself you'll be proud of—sharper, calmer and far more confident than you've ever been.

So, let's begin. We'll start with your **Evening Review Practice**, and then I'll guide you into **Morning Mastery.**

Evening Review

There is no fixed rule for how long your evening review should take. You don't have to follow it like a rigid discipline. Think of it as a friendly check-in with yourself.

I recommend keeping **ten minutes every night before you go to sleep.** If you find it deeply effective and want to add more in the future, make it fifteen. If you're able to do it in five that's perfectly fine too. I'm not imposing a rule; I'm inviting you to build a habit.

To start with, for the first twenty-one days, **give yourself those ten minutes of self-connection.** That's all it takes to begin mastering your days.

Step 1: Reflect

The first step of your evening practice is **Reflection** or you can call it *Review Your Day*. This is your daily check-in, your personal learning time, your nightly reminder that growth happens one day at a time.

Ask yourself three simple questions:

1. **Did I go through my plan today?**
2. **What went right? What went well?**
3. **What could have been better or improved?**

That's it. No judgment, no guilt—just awareness.

This reflection isn't about self-criticism; it's about clarity. When you review your day with honesty, you start to see patterns. You begin to understand your strengths, your blind spots and your distractions. The more clearly you see your day, the more power you have to shape your tomorrow.

When you question yourself daily, you find answers. When you find answers, you bring solutions. And when you bring solutions, you become your own coach.

This is how mastery is built—**not through bursts of motivation, but through daily awareness.** Each night, when you pause to reflect, you reset your direction, appreciate your progress and remind yourself of your purpose.

Of course, there will be days when things don't go as planned. You might get distracted, lose time or face unexpected challenges. That's perfectly fine. Because when you sit down to review, you'll learn what could be avoided, what could be improved and what needs to change.

Transformation doesn't happen in one day; it happens *through* every day. And the simple act of reflecting for ten minutes each night is what accelerates that change.

That's why this step is the foundation of your evening mastery.

Step 2: Plan Your Next Day

Most people plan their day in the morning. They wake up and start thinking, *'What should I do today?'* or *'What's pending?'* And in that half-awake rush—getting ready for office, college or daily chores—the day begins to run *them* instead of *the other way around*.

But here's a simple truth: **If you don't plan your day, you're not planning your life.** Because life is nothing but the sum of all your days.

Mornings are sacred. They're the time when your mind is fresh, creative and filled with willpower. If you spend that precious mental energy figuring out *what* to do, you lose the very fuel you need to *do* it.

That's why I suggest you plan your day the **night before.** When you plan ahead, you wake up with clarity and dive straight into action. This one small shift multiplies your productivity, focus, and peace of mind.

Here's how to do it: Before going to bed, spend a few minutes thinking about your next day and things to do. Write down what matters most and **block specific time slots** for those tasks.

When I say *time-blocking,* I mean literally assigning hours to your priorities. For example, if you're learning a new skill, block **3 p.m. to 5 p.m.** exclusively for it. During that time, silence your phone and give yourself full focus.

Treat that time as sacred, like an appointment with your dreams.

You can do the same for every aspect of life:

- Block time for **deep work** (the tasks that truly move you forward).
- Block time for **emails and messages** (so they don't hijack your day).
- Block time for **relaxation, exercise and social media.**

When you start doing this, you'll notice your days becoming more intentional and your distractions losing power.

Let me share a quick example from my own life. While writing this book, I had multiple things running in parallel—videos to shoot, reels to edit, meetings to attend and business operations to manage. But every single day, I blocked a few hours exclusively for writing. During that time, my phone stayed away and my team knew I was unavailable. Those dedicated blocks turned a busy schedule into focused creation and this book is the result of that discipline.

Remember, **you can't control time but you can control what fills it.** And when you start planning your day the night before, you stop reacting to life and start designing it.

Step 3: Feel Grateful

And now comes the most beautiful part of your evening: **gratitude.**

After you've reflected on your day and planned your tomorrow, take a few quiet moments to *feel thankful*. Not as a ritual, not as another 'to-do', but as a gentle reminder of how much good already exists in your life.

We often end our days thinking about what went wrong—the unfinished tasks, the mistakes, the missed opportunities. But what if you ended your day by noticing what went *right*? That one kind gesture someone showed you, that good meal you enjoyed, that moment of laughter, that peaceful walk or even the fact that you're safe and breathing—all of these are gifts we rarely acknowledge.

Gratitude shifts your focus from *what's missing* to *what's meaningful*. It calms your mind, relaxes your body and gives you the kind of peace that no screen or scroll can offer. When you sleep with a grateful heart, your mind rests easier, your stress lowers and your energy resets.

Science now confirms what ancient wisdom always knew: gratitude rewires your brain. It triggers the release of feel-good hormones like dopamine and serotonin, which not only help you sleep better but also strengthen optimism and resilience.

So, before you close your eyes tonight, pause for just two minutes and silently say 'thank you' for the day you lived, the lessons you learned and the people who make your life brighter. You can even write three things you're grateful for, no matter how big or small.

Some nights it will be something grand, like a major breakthrough. Other nights it might simply be, *'I'm thankful for a good cup of tea'*. Both are equally powerful, because gratitude isn't about the size of the blessing; it's about the awareness of it.

End your day with this feeling, and you'll notice a quiet joy settle within you. And when you wake up the next morning, you'll find yourself naturally more positive, more focused and more ready to act.

That's the magic of gratitude. It not only completes your day, it prepares your tomorrow.

Morning Mastery: Designing Your First Ten Minutes

Just like your evenings help you reflect and reset, your mornings decide the tone of your entire day.

How you begin your morning is how you begin your life because each day is a mini-version of your life.

You don't need an hour-long routine or complicated rituals. Start simple.

Give yourself just ten minutes every morning. If you wish to extend it later, do it gradually. This isn't about how long you sit; it's about how consciously you begin.

Here are three powerful steps to start your day right:

Step 1: Meditate (Start with 5 Minutes)

If you don't already meditate, this is your sign to begin even if it's just for five minutes. Meditation isn't about silencing the mind; it's about *understanding* it. It's about creating a small gap between your thoughts and your reactions.

When you meditate, you train your brain to focus, breathe and pause. That pause is where clarity lives. You'll notice your mornings becoming calmer, your decisions sharper and your reactions more controlled.

You don't need to sit cross-legged on a mountain; you can simply sit comfortably, close your eyes and focus on your breath. If a thought comes, notice it, smile at it and let it pass.

Even five minutes of stillness each morning is enough to change how you show up for the rest of the day.

Step 2: Feel Grateful

You might ask, *'Didn't we already practice gratitude last night?'*

Yes, but this time, the intention is different.

In the evening, gratitude brings peace. In the morning, gratitude brings power.

Starting your day with thankfulness tunes your mind to abundance. It reminds you that you're not beginning from emptiness, you're beginning from fullness.

Before you touch your phone or step into the rush, take a minute to acknowledge three things you're thankful for. It could be something as simple as a new morning, your health, your loved ones or the opportunity to pursue your dreams.

When you start your day on this note, you step into the world with a smile instead of stress. You create a magnetic energy that attracts positivity throughout the day.

Step 3: Visualize and Affirm

We've already discussed the science behind manifestation: how your subconscious mind and the RAS (reticular activating system) respond to what you focus on. Now it's time to make that science your morning habit.

Spend a few minutes **visualizing your goals and affirming your beliefs.** Close your eyes and see yourself living the life you desire. Imagine the details—where you are, how you feel, what you're doing who's around you. Let your emotions align with your vision.

Then, read or recite your affirmations. They are your daily reminders, commands for your subconscious mind. Affirm who you are becoming:

- 'I am confident and calm.'
- 'I attract great opportunities.'
- 'I lead my life with clarity and purpose.'

Feel each word as if it's already true. This combination of visualization and affirmation primes your brain for action. You'll start noticing signs, ideas and chances that align with your goals because your mind is now tuned to find them.

You don't have to do it perfectly. Some days you'll miss it, some days you'll feel distracted. That's okay. The goal isn't perfection; it's *presence*.

So tomorrow morning, give yourself those ten minutes to breathe, to feel, to visualize. And you'll see the difference ripple through your entire day.

Live Your Dreams Every Day

If you've come this far, take a deep breath and smile. You've not just finished a book, you've started a new chapter in your life.

Because everything you've learned—from finding clarity to building belief, from aligning your mind to taking action—leads here, to this simple truth: **transformation doesn't happen in a day; it happens daily.**

Dreams don't come alive through one big leap; they come alive through small, consistent steps taken every single day. Each reflection, each plan, each moment of gratitude, each visualization—they all add up. And one morning, you'll wake up and realize that the life you once visualized is now the life you're living.

That's the power of daily mastery. That's the secret behind every fulfilled person you admire—not luck or magic, but rhythm, reflection and resilience.

You now have everything you need to create the life you desire. You have your clarity. You have your belief. You have your tools to manifest and act. And now, you have a system to sustain it.

So don't wait for the perfect time. Don't wait for motivation or miracles.

Start.

Even if it's for five minutes a day. Even if it's just one action, one affirmation, one step.

Because when you show up for your dreams daily, life begins to show up for you in ways you never imagined.

And years from now, when you look back, you won't remember how hard it was, you'll remember how *worth it* it was.

So, here's my wish for you: May you reflect deeply, believe fiercely, act courageously and live gratefully. May you live your dreams—not someday, but **every day.**

Scan QR code to access the
Penguin Random House India website